To Jeh —
Remember —
God is in the details.

Best of luck and
many blessings
on the occasion of your
swearing in as Secretary
of Homeland Security.

Colleen 12/23/2013

Volumes in the JourneyBook™ Series

On the Way
Vocation, Awareness, and Fly Fishing
Kenneth Arnold

A Priest's Journal
Victor Lee Austin

Yes! We'll Gather at the River!
Barbara Cawthorne Crafton

Confessions of a Fake Priest
Caroline S. Fairless

Notes from a Sojourner
Margaret Guenther

Elijah's Mantle
Pilgrimage, Politics, and Proclamation
Harold T. Lewis

Learning to Love
Gretchen Wolff Pritchard

My Father, My Daughter
Maria Schell and Donald Schell

Praying from the Free-Throw Line—For Now
Minka Shura Sprague

When God Happens
Gray Temple

A Gathering of Gifts
Paula Lawrence Wehmiller

The View from Gabbatha

The View from Gabbatha

MEDITATIONS FROM THE JUDGE'S BENCH

Colleen McMahon

A

JourneyBook ™

from

Church Publishing Incorporated New York

Library of Congress Cataloging-in-Publication Data

McMahon, Colleen,
    The view from Gabbatha : meditations from the judge's bench / by Colleen McMahon.
        p. cm. - (JourneyBook)
    ISBN 0-89869-370-5 (pbk.)
        1. Bible--Meditations. 2. McMahon, Colleen,--Religion. 3. Judges--United
States--Religious life. I. Title. II. Series

BS491.5 .M36 2003
242'.5--dc21

                                                                    2003043849

JourneyBook and colophon are registered trademarks of Church Publishing Incorporated
Designed by Betty Mintz

Church Publishing Incorporated
445 Fifth Avenue
New York, NY 10016

5 4 3 2 1

For George Wade
Best of counselors, best of partners, best of friends.

Colleen McMahon is an active member of the Episcopal Church and former Vice Chancellor of the Diocese of New York. She is the author of *Meditations for Vestry Members*. She lives with her husband and three children.

Foreword

Four years ago, I wrote a book called *Meditations for Vestry Members*. When I got done, I swore that I would never write another book. Then one Sunday, Joan Castagnone from Church Publishing dropped by my parish church. It happened to be a Sunday when I was preaching—on a particularly difficult text, "The Man Who Had a Vineyard" (Lk 20:9–18). The only way I could make sense of that silly parable was to look at its legal aspects. Joan was intrigued by my unorthodox approach; she thought a book of meditations from someone who came at Scripture from an altogether different angle might find an audience. I said yes and started writing. Now that I am finished, I remember why I said I would never write another book. That said, I owe Joan many thanks for the chance to write this one.

The pieces in this book fall into two categories. Some of them are reflections on passages from Scripture, shaped by things that I observe as a lawyer and judge—examples being the essays on the man born blind and Doubting Thomas. I use this technique in the rather unorthodox Sunday school class I teach with my partner in pedagogy, Dr. James Clarke. Jim and I try to convince skeptical adolescents that Scripture can be relevant to their everyday lives. It will come as no surprise (at least, not to our pupils) that I refract Scripture through the prism of my job—even though the Bible was not written with the courtroom in mind.

The other essays are reflections on being a judge. Now I am the first to admit that one does not have to be a person of faith, Christian or otherwise, to be a good judge.

It would violate our Constitution to impose a faith requirement for judges, and I am oath-bound to preserve and protect that sacred document. I take that promise as seriously as any I have ever made. I am, however, convinced that a judge does have to be self-aware, thoughtful and principled to do the job well. Both my principles and my self-awareness (loosely based on the time-honored method called examination of conscience) derive from my faith. So from time to time I train that peculiarly Anglican trifocal lens of Scripture, faith and reason on my thoughts—not my thoughts about questions of law (that, too, would be unconstitutional), but my thoughts about issues like the nature of my oath, a judge's power and responsibility, judicial ethics, and the vexing question of what justice is and ought to be. My spiritual director describes this book as an odd sort of memoir about life on the bench, and I think he is right. I wouldn't be surprised if I keep turning out pieces like these long after this book is published. The act of writing—even writing things no one will ever see—is one of my safety valves. It helps me to keep an eye on myself—a matter, I submit, of some importance to a judge.

In addition to Joan, for her efforts as editor and cheerleader, I am indebted to our mutual friend, the Rev. Elizabeth Searle, who read and commented on the manuscript. Thanks also to my dear friend, the Rev. Canon John Osgood, who was there for me when my batteries ran low or my ideas ran out, and to the Rev. Roger Ferlo, my spiritual director, who writes like I wish I could.

I owe a special debt to someone I have never met—the great Old Testament scholar Walter Brueggemann, whose book, *The Covenanted Self: Explorations in Law and Covenant* (Fortress Press, 1999), has repeatedly provoked and inspired me since I read it three years ago. Brueggemann's book is referenced in a couple of these pieces; it underlies almost every one.

Several of the pieces in this book started as sermons. But for the generosity of two special people, I would have no occasion to write sermons. The first is the Rev. Charles (Chad) Minifie, my rector. For the past seven years, Chad has encouraged me to pursue preaching and given me opportunities to practice the craft he so cherishes. Second is the Rt. Rev. Richard F. Grein, who gave that endeavor his blessing (and who taught me the difference between power and authority—for the reference see the aforementioned "The Man Who Had a Vineyard" on page 49 of this book). Thanks, too, to the Rev. Thomas Nicoll and the people of St. John's Episcopal Church, Larchmont, New York, who have invited me into their pulpit several times.

Finally, to my beloved husband and three wonderful children, I thank you for your patience and understanding—and for letting me have primacy of place on the computer in the study—while I worked on another of what you call my "P.F.L." books.

January 2003

. . . . . .

And he went out and sat on the judge's bench at a place called the
Stone Pavement, which is called in Hebrew Gabbatha.

—John 19:13

IN AN AMERICAN COURTROOM, the bench stands front and center, raised above the well, the focal point. As set design, this does not make a lot of sense. The judge is not the star of the human drama that is played out in the courtroom. The actors in the drama are the combatants—the litigants, their lawyers and the witnesses. These are the parts played by the Tom Cruises and the Meryl Streeps and the Denzel Washingtons. Until the television show *Judging Amy* came along, no play, movie or telecast made a judge a featured player, and for good reason. Her role in the court-room is to listen, not speak; to react, not initiate; to referee, not fight. Or, as I tell my jurors at the beginning of every trial, "I get to wear the costume, and I get the best seat in the house, but I am the least important person here, because the lawyers and the witnesses do the work, and you make the decision."

So why, exactly, is the bench the focal point of the courtroom? Well, for one thing, it reflects political reality. Western justice developed in societies where the king was the final arbiter of disputes. The king, of course, sits on a high seat, as a matter of precedence and power. Since the judge dispenses the king's justice, the judge sits in the place of the king—that is, in the high place.

The position of the bench also underscores the judge's neutrality. By sitting in the highest place, she is above the fray, and thus better able to bring calm, dispassionate reason to bear on a contentious, not to mention tense, situation.

But there is more. In our religious tradition, an omniscient God is the ultimate judge. We place that God "in the heavens"—that is, in a high place, from which he can take in everything at a glance. This, presumably, gives him a terrific vantage point for meting out what each of us deserves. Well, from the raised bench, a judge sees everything that goes on in his courtroom far more clearly than anyone else can. It gives a different perspective on things. I have been a judge for more than seven years, and I can attest that things look different from the bench than they do to the litigants, the attorneys, the witnesses, the spectators, the politicians and the press.

My view from the bench colors a lot more than what I see in the courtroom. Some people rail at the thought that they are what they do, but I don't believe that human beings are particularly good at compartmentalization. The strands of our lives are so tightly interwoven that what we do cannot help but influence who we are, and how we see and feel and react to everything that goes on around us. So I guess it doesn't surprise me that my occupation affects the way I read the Bible, or that my musings on the Word of God have taken on a decidedly judicial cast.

I first recognized this when a new spiritual director asked me to reflect on the story of Zaccheus—the little tax collector who shinnied up a tree to get a better look at Jesus. When I reported back, the tale had taken on a definite courtroom flavor. I don't remember all the details—if I did, it would be a piece in this book—but I do recall imagining that Zaccheus looked like Danny De Vito, and that his dinner table conversation with Jesus sounded something like the exchange I might have at the sentencing of a remorseful public servant who had been caught with his hand in the till. A few months later, while listening to the Gospel for Low Sunday (Doubting Thomas), I found myself ruminating on the relative probative value of direct evidence ("Unless I see the nail marks in his hands and feet, I will not believe.") versus circumstantial evidence ("Do you believe because you have seen? Blessed are they who have not seen yet have believed!"). After only a few months on the job, I had experienced a profound transformation in my point of reference. When I heard or read Scripture, phrases or passages brought to mind matters of law, and as I confronted disputes and decisions, biblical quotations suggested themselves to me. That has continued, as you will see from the meditations and sermons that follow, all of which were written after I became a judge. They reflect my new perspective: The View From Gabbatha.

When I shared that working title with my spiritual director, he said, "Whoa, that's heavy!" I understand his reaction. Gabbatha is not a place of justice in the Christian tradition. It is the Stone Pavement at the Antonia Fortress in Jerusalem. It is the place from which Pilate pronounced Jesus' doom. It is the site of history's most notoriously unjust verdict, uttered by history's most wrong-headed jurist. And yet I am comfortable with the metaphor.

The word "justice" carries such sacred connotations. People of many cultures share a belief that Objective Right and Objective Wrong exist, and that the Embodiment of Righteousness will somehow ensure that virtue is rewarded while the wicked get their just deserts. In "justice" are overtones of Eden and Sinai and the End Times. Heavy stuff indeed.

But when I sit on the bench, I am neither the deity dispensing justice nor some Solomon blessed with a special quotient of wisdom. I am a human being, trying to make sense of confrontations that are not of my making. And I am buffeted by the same forces that acted on Pilate on that Friday morning long ago: law that is not always clear; righteous litigants driven by unstated agendas; false friends and turncoats; witnesses who may or may not be truth-tellers; personal tragedy; popular will; political reality; and strange people who cannot or will not explain themselves to me. You can't sit on any judge's bench without sharing the View from Gabbatha. It comes with the job.

But that does not mean every judge behaves like Rome's most infamous procurator. Most people who sit on the bench embody virtues we never associate with Pilate: they are thoughtful, careful, decisive, independent, and models of probity. Becoming that kind of judge—a judge who keeps one eye on his conscience while fixing the other firmly on the law—takes some effort. My way of attacking the problem is to cultivate another perspective—looking at what I do through the prism of my faith. As for whether I have succeeded in keeping my inner Pilate at bay, you can be the judge.

. . . . . .

...that they may discern the truth, and impartially administer the law in the fear of thee alone....
—Collect for Courts of Justice, Book of Common Prayer

IN THE BACK OF THE BOOK OF COMMON PRAYER you can find prayers for all occasions—an inestimable help to those who have a hard time improvising. I found Collect 21, For Courts of Justice, just as I was starting my judicial career. I printed it out and taped it to the lip of the bench. I can see those words, "In the fear of thee alone," every time I look down. This is a good thing, because being a judge can be very hard.

Most people think that it would be terrific to be a judge—you have interesting and varied work, you control your schedule (more or less), you are the object of respect, you are in charge. I don't deny that I like these aspects of the job—not the least because scientists tell us that people who are in charge and who have control over their professional lives tend to live longer and remain more active as they age (now I understand why there are so many old judges).

But terrific doesn't mean easy. Few people reckon with the need for courage. It was what surprised me the most about the job once I finally got it. As a judge, you are constantly on view. You know that every decision you make adds to the reputation you are building—among lawyers, among court personnel, among more senior judges, among the members of the press who cover your cases. Face it, we all

. . . . . .

want people to think well of us. And reputation matters. Some judges have to be reelected. Some have to be reappointed. Some who need not fear losing their jobs, thanks to life tenure, aspire to sit on a higher court.

So the temptation to appeal to the court of public opinion is always there and always potent. But it must be resisted at all costs. The judge's job is to make the legally correct decision, not the popular one. No matter what they say on TV, it's not supposed to be The People's Court.

How does one resist the forces that buffet us just as they did Pilate 2,000 years ago? Well, the key is where we choose to focus our attention. If we look inward, focusing on ourselves, or outward, toward the opinions of others, we will fail. We need to look up, to something mysterious and centering and beyond our reach. The poet Robert Frost put it thus in his poem, "Choose Something Like a Star":

> So when at times the mob is swayed
> to carry praise or blame too far,
> We may choose something, like a star,
> To stay our minds on, and be staid.

The star, being above and beyond us, "demands of us a certain height," as Frost observed. Otherwise we could not reach for it. A good judge who is reaching for justice looks beyond herself and others, and so beyond the lure of self-regard and public opinion.

. . . . . .

The Bible addresses this. When Jethro, Moses' father-in-law, suggested that the overworked prophet hand off the task of adjudicating minor disputes, he was quite specific about what was required: "Able men among all the people, men who fear God, are trustworthy, and hate dishonest gain" (Ex 18:21). Societies quite properly worry about whether the men and women who become judges are able and honest. But while our Constitution does not permit us to require that judges fear God, I have come to believe that fear of the Lord is a valuable commodity in a judge. Being centered on something above and beyond myself is every bit as important to the job as all the ability and honesty in the world.

The proof of the pudding is the coward who sat on the real Gabbatha. Pilate did not look up. He looked in and out, and let his personal ambition override his impersonal judgment. Pilate's sole concern was what people—the mob, the Emperor—would think of him. "If you let this man go, you are no friend of Caesar," cries the crowd in John's Gospel; and when Pilate heard these words, he sat on the judgment seat and gave them what they wanted—no matter that he found no fault in the man who stood before him (Jn 19:12–16). This hardly qualifies as an exercise of judgment. Luke, too, strips away the pretense that Pilate was acting as a jurist; his Pilate "gave his verdict that their demand should be granted," and committed the monstrous crime of executing an innocent man (Lk 23:24). Pilate asked, "What is truth?" The truth is that Pilate perverted the system of justice by preferring the public's verdict to the right one. So, too, does any judge who listens to any voice except the inner one that, after study of the precedents and reflection on the facts and consultation

. . . . . .

with clerks or colleagues, tells him the right way to administer the laws.

Fortunately for our society, most of the men and women who sit on the bench do not read the newspapers looking for answers. "Justice is not blind" is the cynicism of the moment. It's not even a new cynicism; over a century ago, Chicago newspaperman Peter Finley Dunne held the same jaundiced view about judicial independence that the press does today. His alter ego, Mr. Dooley, once remarked that the Supreme Court seemed able to follow the newspapers.

Unfortunately, that is a dangerous notion in a society built on respect for the law. And, while it is largely a calumny, it has seeped into our national consciousness and affected the process of judge making in an insidious way, turning what ought to be a dispassionate search for Jethro's honest and wise arbiter into an ideological battle. The judges I know are not ideologues: they call them as they see them, not as politicians or the press demands. All judges have personal opinions and political views. But very few of us go to work each day with the goal of vindicating some private agenda. Whether consciously or not, the judges I know are centered on something outside themselves. Call it God, call it a star, call it some abstract ideal of justice—call it what you will. We really want to do the right thing.

My star is the star of Bethlehem; my magic words are, "In the fear of thee alone." I read them whenever I look down. I whisper them to myself ten times a day. They are my prayer, my plea, my cry from out of the depths—a cry that I may never stop reaching for the heights where true justice can be found. O Lord, hear my calling.

· · · · · ·

Who gives speech to mortals?....Now go, and I will be with your mouth and teach you what you are to speak.

—Exodus 4:11–12

WHEN I WAS A TEENAGER, I wanted to be a Broadway star in the worst way. And I wanted to sound like a Broadway star, too. So I sang in my chest voice, belting out everything from the scores of my favorite musical comedies to the awful post-Vatican II folk rock that had replaced my beloved Gregorian chants in church. I was not a bad belter. But it was not my true voice.

I did not begin to find my true voice until I started singing in my church choir. I had not sung seriously in eighteen years, but I had joined our church for its excellent music, so the new organist's open call for singers was irresistible. Still, I could not just pick up where I left off, because there was no room in my church choir for the heavy chest voice I had cultivated during my starstruck years. The conductor, a former boy chorister, wanted as clear, pure, "white" a sound as grown women could give him. So I began to look for that voice. It was elusive; years of misuse, followed by years of nonuse, meant that I had no idea where my real range lay or what my natural, unforced tone quality sounded like.

I began working with a voice teacher. Slowly, carefully, he unlocked my throat. We discovered there notes I had no idea I could sing, and a light, lovely tone no one knew I possessed. As time passed, I gradually transformed myself from a belter

. . . . . .

into the singer I was genetically programmed to be, with a voice that was ideal for chant, Renaissance polyphony, and the music of composers like Britten, Howells, and especially Bach. To my very great regret, the voice I ended up with was less than ideal for performing other music I liked, including American pop standards and hit songs from Broadway shows. But I had to give up that voice—the voice I wanted—in order to get the voice God meant for me to have. As I got used to it, I saw that, like all God's gifts, my true voice was good. I am glad I found it.

I also had to work to find the right voice to use when I became a judge. I practiced law for almost twenty years before I went on the bench. The feisty yet persuasive voice of the litigator came easily to me. When I first went on the bench I did not look too hard for a different voice, and a number of my early opinions read more like partisan briefs than impartial statements. I was repeating my musical error in my professional life; the voice I was using was the wrong voice for my new role.

But there is a real judge's voice behind the trial lawyer's bombast, and I am growing into it, just as I grew into my soprano. From time to time, I still want to jump over the bench and mix it up with the lawyers in the old way, but that happens less frequently than it used to. It is becoming more natural to speak in a voice that sounds less edgy and more above the fray. It takes a lot of practice, but more and more I am getting it right.

We tend to imagine that Jesus always spoke in his true voice. But I don't think he did. I have come to believe that Jesus, like every other human being, had to work hard in order to develop his true voice, and that he shed some preconceptions along the way.

I reached this conclusion while teaching the Gospel of Mark to my seventh and eighth grade Sunday school class. The students were particularly intrigued by the story about Jesus' putting the demons into the pigs, who promptly ran off the cliff and drowned. They thought that was a pretty silly and hurtful thing for Jesus to do. And, two chapters later, they were horrified by his comment to the Syrophoenician woman—you know, the one where Jesus refuses to cure her daughter, saying that it wasn't fair to give the children's food to the dogs. As soon as they figured out that the Jews were the children and everyone else was a dog, my students decided that Jesus was no better than David Duke. That did not jibe with the vision of their Savior they had been handed since childhood. It also didn't jibe with what the rector and their parents thought I was teaching them.

I felt compelled to make sense of these two strange stories, if only for the students' benefit. Eventually, I concluded that they represented two stopping points along Jesus' journey of self-discovery. Mark's Jesus did not think twice about condemning those pigs to death. But why should he? Jews held that pigs were unclean. So, in theory, the world was better off without them. Certainly the man who donated his demons to the swine was better off. As for the poor swineherd and his family, who lost everything when those possessed piggies jumped off the cliff like so many lemmings—well, he could not have been a Jew, since Jews did not raise pigs. So his feelings were of no account.

. . . . . .

It was hard for me to think of Jesus in this way. But the human being Jesus was a product of his time and place. He was a Jew, one of a people who believed God had set them apart from others and who lived accordingly, despite the increasingly cosmopolitan nature of their world. He had been trained from childhood not to associate with outsiders. He had been trained from childhood to think them unclean. His ministry, at least at that point, was to his own people and no one else. To imagine that he did not have the same sensibilities as his family and friends—none of whom would have given a fig for a man who raised pigs—is to divorce him from his context, and ultimately from his humanity. It must have been a hard intellectual and spiritual journey for Jesus to find the voice that we hear when we read his words—a voice more universal than that of the Hebrew prophets he revered, a voice that ran counter to the culture in which he was immersed.

The Syrophoenician woman is one of my favorite characters in the Gospels, because her role in Jesus' life was to help him come to the realization that he had not yet found his true voice. She takes on Jesus on his own terms—okay, prophet man, you think my daughter and I are dogs, we'll be dogs—and she goes one better with his own analogy, by reminding him that dogs can always survive on the crumbs that fall from the children's table. In my imagination, Jesus hears her words and has an epiphany, a sudden realization that the doctrine of love and repentance he has been preaching could have a whole new layer of meaning. At the precise moment when he admits that she has a point—"For saying that, you may go—the demon has left your daughter." (Mk 7:29)—he begins to understand that his message could also be for people who are not part of his culture, people who really have no call on him. This is a significant step on Jesus' road from tribal prophet to universal visionary, from the voice he thought he wanted to the voice God always intended to put in his mouth.

Anyone who is to have voice must find the right voice—-his true voice—or what he says will only be so much hot air. Jesus was not exempt from that rule, and his words are more precious to me because of it.

· · · · · ·

Thou shalt not bear false witness against thy neighbor.
—Exodus 20:16 (The Ninth Commandment)

WHEN MY SEVENTH AND EIGHTH GRADE Sunday school class studied the baptismal promise about resisting evil and repenting from sin, I asked everyone to identify something that was evil. The students came up with shoplifting, vandalism, teasing, assault, war, even adultery. But not one pre-teen mentioned lying—not even my son, who has been taught from the cradle that telling a lie is the ultimate sin. After class, I began to wonder whether I, as a judge, ought to be concerned about this omission.

I am concerned about it. From where I sit, nothing is more important than telling the truth. And I think that, as a society, we do not appreciate the importance of truth as much as we used to.

In my courtroom, everything stops whenever anyone—a witness, a potential juror, even a bailiff—takes the oath. For the brief duration of that ceremony, my entire attention is fixed on the person being sworn. I expect everyone else's to be as well. In other courtrooms I have visited, the oath may be accompanied by paper shuffling, spectators walking in and out, the movement of clerks—but not in mine. There is no more sacred moment in a trial than the moment when someone swears to tell the whole truth and nothing but. I refuse to let it pass unremarked.

My fascination with truth telling is not of recent vintage. For reasons I cannot

· · · · · ·

fathom, when I was in the third grade, my favorite Bible story was Susannah and the Elders. Its more lurid aspects escaped me—the only "lying" I knew about was telling a lie, so I didn't have a clue what the Elders wanted when they asked Susannah to "lie" with them (of course, in those days I also thought "adultery" was the sin of being an adult). But I rejoiced when the perjuring Elders got their deadly due. My mother had told me that lying was the worst thing I could ever do, and also the silliest, because the truth would always come out. The fate of the Elders at Daniel's hand proved her correct.

I am no longer so naive. I know that an oath is not an insurance policy. People swear to tell the truth and then sit down in the witness chair and lie their asses off. God knows I have heard more untruths told under oath than you can possibly imagine—people who are trying to get themselves out of chancery, or out of jail, invent the most wildly implausible stories and stick to them through thick and thin, even if they look like fools in the eyes of everyone who hears them. Withering cross-examination that would make Perry Mason proud cannot shake them. Even more tragic: an increasing number of our fellow citizens have come to believe that certain classes of people—police officers, government officials, doctors, business executives—lie routinely while on the witness stand. While I hold that "testilying" is more the exception than the rule, it does happen. Whether it leads to the conviction of an innocent person, makes it easier to put a guilty one away or helps someone avoid civil liability is irrelevant. What is relevant is that the oath is meaningless to some of the people who take it. And, contrary to what my

. . . . . .

mother told me, the truth does not always come out. Some liars don't get caught.

This is a tragedy. The oath has always been a sacred thing. The ninth commandment—"Thou shalt not bear false witness against thy neighbor"—does not proscribe lying in general, as I was taught years ago. It is squarely aimed at one particular kind of lie: perjury in a lawsuit ("bearing false witness") against another member of the covenant community ("my neighbor"). The great Old Testament scholar Walter Brueggemann once observed that Israel's preservation depended on the validity of the judgments rendered by the judges who were its first governors. It was imperative that those judgments be, to use Brueggemann's words, "honest and reliable and untainted by interest." So the utmost solemnity attended the giving of testimony. One bore witness before the priests and judges, which is to say, before the Lord (Deut 19:17). So great was the sin of false attestation that the Deuteronomist wrote,

> If the witness is a false witness, having testified falsely against another, then you shall do to the false witness just as the false witness had meant to do to the other. So shall you purge the evil from your midst. The rest shall hear and be afraid, and a crime such as this shall never again be committed among you. Show no pity: life for life, eye for eye, tooth for tooth, hand for hand, foot for foot.
>
> (Deuteronomy 19:18–21)

Hence the fate of the Elders in my favorite Bible story. When Susannah rebuffed their advances, they accused her of adultery, the sentence for which was death. Once Daniel exposed their lie, the old goats were promptly executed.

Show no pity to the perjurer. It is not the killer or the thief but the liar who threatens the viability of the community. It sounds kind of fire-and-brimstone-y, this Hamurabi-esque vision of justice for perjurers—especially in a country that recently endured a national debate about whether certain kinds of perjury in certain kinds of lawsuits are important enough to worry about. Such a debate could never have taken place in ancient Israel, where perjury was unjustifiable because it tore at the fabric of society.

And who is my neighbor, as a lawyer was once heard to ask a prophet? Originally, that neighbor was any other member of the covenant community formed at Sinai. Well, America, too, is a covenant community. Our very existence depends on widespread respect for and obedience to the law. In the United States, as in no other country on earth, confidence in the courts underlies the social compact. Yes, we are a litigious people, but that is because most of us believe that justice is to be found in the courts rather than on the streets. Judgments that are honest and reliable and uncontaminated by interest are no less an imperative to America than they were to biblical Israel.

I happen to know the power of the oath from both sides, because I have testified in a lawsuit. I have stood in a witness box and been sworn. I have held up my right hand and promised to tell the whole truth and nothing but. I was giving pretty

. . . . . .

technical evidence—there's nothing juicy or salacious about the negotiation of a settlement agreement. Still, the whole time, I was conscious that I was not just talking about these matters. I was testifying. I was always aware of the oath. It preyed on my mind. While I was answering one question, a detail that was responsive to an earlier question popped into my head. I immediately backtracked to amplify my earlier answer. Had I committed perjury by omitting that detail the first time around? Certainly not; I had answered the first question fully and honestly while it was on the table. But I had promised to tell the whole truth and nothing but, so when this new factoid bubbled up from my subconscious, I felt I had to reveal it. The oath demanded it.

I believe that mostly truth is told in American courtrooms, because I believe that most witnesses feel as I felt when they raise their rights hands. They think, as I think, that the oath is sacred, and solemn, and important. It wields a power over us, whether we think so in the abstract or not. I cannot know this to be true; like my faith in God, my belief in the power of the oath is a hope in a thing unseen. But I could not do my job if I did not have this hope.

That is why there is no such thing as a inconsequential lie in an American court of law. That is why the oath is our jurisprudential sacrament. When it is administered, attention must be paid.

Jesus took with him Peter and James and John, and led them up a high mountain...and he was transfigured before them.

—Mark 9:2

I WAS HAPPY AS A PRACTICING LAWYER, and young women lawyers, for whom I seem to be a role model, often ask me why. I think that my secret is that I always found it easy to be one of the guys. Maybe it came from growing up in a large family. I thrived on the camaraderie. I loved the late nights, the pizza and Chinese food consumed in conference rooms, and the sense of "We're all in this together" that intensified as discovery deadlines loomed, or briefs came due, or trial dates drew near. We worked hard together for days on end and played hard together whenever we got a break. We were more than colleagues. We shared hopes and dreams and secrets in an atmosphere that was one part professional office and one part summer camp or college dorm. We became confidantes, as you can only with people whom you know, and who know you, really well. It was the best part of practicing law.

It helped that I was at a law firm where everyone, from the most senior partner to the newest clerical employee, was called by first name. Lack of formality contributes mightily to a "Band of Brothers" atmosphere. At Paul Weiss Rifkind Wharton & Garrison, formality was reserved for the clients. Younger lawyers respected their elders, but the best senior associates and partners understood that there was a professional advantage if neophytes felt that they were thought of as professionals. So they consciously cultivated an atmosphere in which elder-worship was discouraged and teamwork encouraged. In that atmosphere, the people who thrived were the ones who loved being one of the guys.

The worst part about being a judge is that you simply cannot be one of the guys. From the minute you don that black robe, people look at you differently. They treat you with what they would characterize as respect, and what I characterize as a certain reserve, often laced with a perceptible dose of sucking up. It's hard to explain, but you sort of meld with the office—not really, of course, but in people's eyes—to the point where one judge I know actually refers to herself as "the robe." Someone once said that you'd better have a lot of friends before you go on the bench, because you won't make any new ones afterward. He knew whereof he spoke. People simply will not allow themselves to get close to you. Even your old friends behave toward you in subtly different ways. I had not counted on that.

The mark of my isolation is that my first name has changed from "Colleen" to "Judge." Whenever I am introduced to someone—even at a cocktail party or at a meeting at my children's school—it is as "Judge McMahon." Now, I suppose that is inevitable when you barely know the person who is making the introduction, but my closest friends, my old partners, do it, too. And when they do, it sounds even more pompous and off-putting: "I'd like you to meet Colleen McMahon—I mean *Judge* McMahon." They sound for all the world like they think I will be offended if they don't attach a title to me—me, the one who thrived on the fellowship that was epitomized by our use of first names. I have given up trying to fight it, however, because

. . . . . .

I've learned that I can't win. Now that I am a judge, I have been transfigured.

At first the change in people's behavior toward me drove me crazy. It still makes me uncomfortable. I liked being one of the guys, and I miss it. But I have come to understand that the distance I find so personally discomfiting helps me do my job "without fear or favor" as required by my oath. The fact that people will not let themselves get too close protects me from allegations of partiality. I hear stories from time to time about clients who think their lawyers will get special privileges or better results from some judge, because the judge likes the lawyers personally or respects them professionally. I find these stories at once amusing (because it shows how little the clients know about most judges) and upsetting (for the lawyers, who don't deserve the insinuation that they are influence peddlers). But they do circulate. Better that I just avoid the problem altogether.

The Transfiguration occupies a pivotal place in the Synoptic Gospels. Before it, Jesus was the leader of a motley crew of friends, who worked together and studied together and traveled together and ate together and camped together. Of course, even before his garments became whiter than snow, there were things about Jesus that set him apart from his closest followers. But he also told one hell of a story and enjoyed a good feed—both qualities that make for a valued friend. Nothing in Matthew, Mark or Luke suggests that Jesus was not able to be one of the guys with the apostles. I like to imagine him with his buddies, doing the silly things that friends do—having a drink at the end of a hard day, sharing jokes around the campfire, hiding each others' sandals, sharing a blanket on a cold night.

. . . . . .

The Transfiguration changed all that. After they came down from the mountain, Jesus could no longer be one of the guys, because now his friends knew, irrefutably, that he was *not* one of the guys. Jesus' friends couldn't possibly have treated their buddy in the same old way after seeing him clothed in light, talking with giants and legends. I'll bet they started calling him "Master" or "Rabbi," all the time, even when outsiders were not around. They probably took a little extra care with his gear, and stopped playing practical jokes when he was around, and started doing his share of the chores. All of this inevitably put distance between him and his friends. It's too bad. A little of the old camaraderie in those last weeks of Jesus' journey might have gone a long way toward alleviating the pain of what was to come.

Or maybe not. My own transfiguration lacked the special effects of Jesus on the mountaintop, but it had its own shock value; it forced me to turn my full attention to the new work that I had to do. I think it was a necessary—even pivotal—part of growing into my vocation, of "becoming" a judge. Maybe the Transfiguration of the Gospels was similarly necessary. Maybe it happened in order to put some distance between Jesus and the human beings to whom he was closest, to loosen one of the few bonds that tied this man to this world he was supposed to save. As long as he could be one of the guys, Jesus had a reason to postpone the great and difficult task that lay before him. Once that lure was removed, the work became paramount. In the Synoptics, no sooner is Jesus transfigured than he turns his face toward Jerusalem. It was the sign that he had to fulfill his vocation. If Jesus couldn't be one of the guys, there was nothing for it but to die.

. . . . . .

Blessed are those who have not seen and yet have come to believe.
—John 20:29

ONE OF MY JOBS is to enforce the rules of evidence. Some forms of proof can be introduced at trial while others cannot. The rules are highly technical and seem silly, or even counter-intuitive, to many people (including judges and lawyers, at least some of the time). But they arose because our legal system deems some types of information not sufficiently reliable to serve as the basis for a verdict.

There are shorthand names for this inherently unreliable evidence: we exclude proof that is "irrelevant," "inauthentic" and "prejudicial." Perhaps the most familiar of those evidentiary buzzwords is "hearsay." All viewers of courtroom dramas know that we do not allow juries to base verdicts on "hearsay."

Now, hearsay has a very specific definition. It is an out-of-court statement of fact that is offered to prove the truth of the matter asserted. Easy example: assume that Barbara is accused of bank robbery. At her trial, John cannot get on the witness stand and say, "Mary told me that she saw Barbara rob the bank." That is because the source of the incriminating information is Mary, not John; he wasn't there and he only knows what he heard second-hand. So it's Mary's reliability as a witness, not John's, that needs to be tested through cross-examination.

We exclude hearsay because experience teaches us that when something really important is on the line, the best evidence comes from those who actually saw, heard, or experienced the incidents about which testimony must be given. You don't have to be a lawyer to know the truth in this hoary rule: which of us has not played Telephone, dissolving in laughter when we learn how the whispered message changed as it passed from ear to ear. At the end of the game, we have to go back to the person who started the message in the first place in order to be sure what was said. Everyone else's version is hearsay.

Nothing is more important to Christians than their faith in the Jesus of the creeds: the man who preached ultimate truth, worked impossible miracles, died a horrible death—and came back to life. So it's more than a little ironic that we base our belief on evidence that would never be admitted in a court of law. The Gospels are replete with hearsay. In fact, to the extent they purport to recount history, the Gospels are hearsay. They were written between forty and eighty years after the events they describe. While they are attributed to people who knew Jesus, they were in fact written by people who never met the man—people who heard Jesus' story from other people, who might have heard it from an eyewitness. They are demonstrably unreliable about many things. They are inconsistent with each other on key points, like when during his ministry Jesus overturned the money-changers' tables, and who saw what on Easter Day, and where and when Jesus last met with his apostles. They contain errors of time, place and historical fact.

It gets worse. Over the centuries, the Gospels broke free of their original cultural moorings and traveled around the world. In the process, many references that early hearers of the stories would have understood and appreciated became obscure and had to be recast in terms that a new audience would comprehend. Each new translation or layer of interpretation meant that something of Jesus and his message could be lost or distorted. The dark underside of Christian history—murderous Crusades, Inquisitions, anti-Semitism—demonstrates that something was indeed lost in this two-thousand-year game of Telephone.

So—objection to the Gospels as proof that Jesus is the Risen Lord sustained. But should it be? After all, there are a number of well-settled exceptions to the hearsay rule. Does any of the evidence in the Gospels fit within them? As a matter of fact, it does.

For example, we admit "excited utterances." These are exclamations made under conditions so stressful that they afford the speaker no time to reflect—statements like Mary Magdalene's "Rabboni!" whispered as she recognizes that a dead man is standing before her and calling her name, or the beloved disciple's "It is the Lord!" shouted at the strangely familiar man cooking breakfast on the beach. And we let juries consider "present sense impressions": words uttered at the very moment someone witnesses an unusual event, such as Peter's offer to build three tents for Jesus, Moses and Elijah during the Transfiguration. We also admit statements that were, at the time they were made, so far contrary to the speaker's interest that no reasonable person would have said such a thing unless it were true: Saul of Tarsus, persecutor of The Way, rising from the Damascus Road and proclaiming, "He is the Son of God" to hostile crowds in the synagogues. Then there's my personal favorite Biblical hearsay exception: Jesus' Easter afternoon query, "Have you anything to eat?"

It comes within the exception for statements about the speaker's existing mental, emotional or physical condition.

There is also a catchall exception to the hearsay rule. We permit juries to consider hearsay when we have independent guarantees that an out-of-court statement is more likely true than not true. I submit that such guarantees of the Gospels' trustworthiness—not as historical fact, but as theological truth—do indeed exist. Consider the miraculous fact that the teachings of an itinerant Palestinian who lived two thousand years ago undergird much of modern Western thought. Or that this seemingly unimportant person from an unimportant corner of an ancient world inspired some of the most extraordinary creative outpourings—literary, musical, artistic—that have ever emanated from the human soul. Or that the stories about his life, death and resurrection—regardless of their historical accuracy or logical plausibility—continued to resonate with men and women, regardless of where and when they lived, despite repeated efforts by a skeptical world to expose the hero as a fraud or his followers as superstitious.

The rabbi Gamaliel told the Sanhedrin that if this new movement were of human origin it would fail (Acts 5:33–39). His words were accounted wise, and they still ring true. None of the facts I have listed makes sense as the world measures sense. But every one of them is true. If the existence of such improbabilities does not sufficiently guarantee the fundamental trustworthiness of the good news of God in Jesus, then nothing short of another face-to-face encounter with the Risen Lord would suffice.

. . . . . .

Unfortunately, those of us who were not privileged to be in the garden in Jerusalem, or the beach at Tiberias, or on the road to Damascus cannot expect any such encounter. Jesus made that clear enough when he appeared to a skeptic of his own time—to Thomas, who was elsewhere on the first day of the new era in human history. Thomas demanded some non-hearsay evidence of this astonishing development before he would accept it. "Have you believed because you have seen me? Blessed are those who have not seen and yet have come to believe," said the Lord. That's us—those who have not seen. If we believe, it can only be because the hearsay evidence—unreliable though it be, distorted though some have made it—still contains a kernel of immutable truth. We, the members of the jury, recognize that kernel, and with our verdict declare it to be true.

And who is he, sir? Tell me, that I may believe in him.

—John 9:36

AT THE END OF EVERY TRIAL, I remind my jurors that people witnessing the same event from different vantage points may see or hear it differently.

After over seven years as a trial judge, I know whereof I speak. Different people do see the same evidence differently. I take a professional interest in this phenomenon, because as a judge I notice it all the time. My favorite example: I once presided at the trial of a union executive who was accused of embezzling funds. To me, after years of representing big corporations, it looked like a not terribly egregious case of expense account padding at the union's rather lavish annual convention. I had seen far worse, and so couldn't even figure out why the case had been indicted. I was flabbergasted when the jury returned a verdict that required me to put the fellow in jail for years. Then I spoke with the jurors. Seven of the twelve belonged to unions, and they were in shock. "Judge, we had no idea that was what the big-wigs did with our union dues!" Clearly, they brought very different perceptions to the trial than I did.

The Gospel story about the curing of the man born blind is very much about differences in perception and how those differences affect our judgments. The question the story raises is fundamental: who is this Jesus? Everyone in the story asks that question, and evaluates it in light of a single piece of evidence: a man is cured of his blindness. Yet they do not reach a unanimous verdict.

. . . . . .

Now, when a trial gets to the point where jurors who have heard the same testimony cannot reach a verdict, we ask them to step back from their own beliefs and try to stand in the shoes of the jurors whose views differ from theirs. So let's see if we can understand how the participants in this Gospel story look at the evidence.

The man born blind voices no doubts: Jesus is a prophet from God. And he makes a powerful case. Jesus touched his eyes, and now the man can see. Who else could Jesus be?

At first blush, this would appear to be the best evidence. After all, the man is giving personal witness. Yet he convinces only himself, not the neighbors or the Pharisees. I submit this was for reasons all of us can readily understand. The man's experience of God was powerful, but it was deeply personal, not communal. Jesus had not touched anyone else's eyes. It's hard to draw conclusions based only on someone else's deeply personal experience. So the testimony of the man born blind, while powerful, was far less convincing to the neighbors and the Pharisees than it was to him.

The neighbors don't know how to interpret the evidence. Now, don't you find that strange? After all, the man born blind was a given in their lives. The neighbors saw him every single day, wrapped in his ragged clothes, seated on the ground, holding out his bowl, like some pesky Palestinian squeegee man. Who was better positioned to reach a favorable conclusion about Jesus than the neighbors?

But they don't. Far from being persuaded that Jesus has revealed God's glory, the neighbors are confused—so confused that they question what their eyes tell them is true, saying really dopey things like, "No, it is not he; it is someone like him," even though they know that no one who looks like the blind beggar has been hanging around the neighborhood.

I think this can only be because the cure challenges the neighbors' settled expectations, which play more of a role in our lives than we realize. The thing that was a given in the neighbors' lives was a *blind* beggar. Now that there is no more blind beggar, there is no more given. Until someone can make sense of this unusual event, the neighbors will be suspicious, and view the evidence about Jesus as inconclusive.

The Pharisees, who were brought on the scene to clear up the neighbors' confusion, are also confused, at least at first. But confusion is the enemy to these men. Remember who the Pharisees are: not a group of zealous bigots, as Christian children have long been taught, but religious scholars who were trying to retain a sense of Israel as a separate nation in a world where an all-powerful empire wants to assimilate everyone. The Pharisees cannot tolerate confusion about ultimate matters; they have to reach some conclusion about what is going on. Naturally, they look at the evidence in the context of their mission of maintaining the integrity of the community. And they apply to that evidence a logic that grows out of their belief system.

Viewed from that perspective, their conclusion that Jesus is a tool of the devil is perfectly logical. The Pharisees are trying to keep the Chosen People true to their special calling in a world of false messiahs. Some people are calling Jesus the Messiah. But he does not happen to fit the community's preconception of who its

· · · · · ·

deliverer will be. Jesus himself is sending out mixed signals. In his favor, he is highly charismatic and he has performed miraculous deeds of the sort one might expect from The One Who Is To Come. But he has also created havoc in the Temple, the visible symbol of Jewish belief and identity, and made blasphemous claims about himself, saying, "Before Abraham came to be, I AM (Jn 8:58)."

In the blind man's cure, the Pharisees see Jesus' two faces. That a man who was once blind can now see is powerful evidence that Jesus comes from God. But it is not dispositive. As some Pharisees pointed out, maguses and conjurers can perform tricks, too. So the Pharisees look at the context of the cure. There they find highly persuasive evidence. Jesus broke the Sabbath to give the blind man his sight. This seems to us a technicality, but to them it's no light matter. The Jews have no statues or banners to symbolize their identity: Shabbat Shalom, Sabbath rest, is the visible symbol of their status as a people who remain separate and recognizable in a world overrun by Romans. A Jew who works on the Sabbath breaches the wall that keeps the covenant community safe from the taint of those who do not recognize the One True God. The Pharisees conclude that Jesus is from the devil, not because they are blind to the obvious, but because they are not blind to what is obvious to them: the Jewish people's fragile identity as a community will be torn asunder if the rules are bent too far.

So we have in this story three different views of who Jesus is, coming from three different vantage points: one informed by personal experience, one informed by a confounding of expectations, and one informed by the desire for communal survival.

. . . . . .

No one looks at the evidence in the same way because everyone comes at the evidence from a different place. No wonder they can't come up with the same answer.

All of us have to answer the question of who Jesus is, in history and in our own lives. What perspective do we bring to the evidence we find in the Gospels?

Well, I imagine that most of us were baptized as babies and grew up in Christian households, imbibing Christian stories and views of the world. If you are like me, you probably reached adulthood with pretty settled expectations about Jesus. I thought he conformed to the comfortable images I grew up with: as gentle and meek, the babe in the manger, the Good Shepherd. He was a refuge, not a challenge; a friend, not a goad.

But when I studied the Gospels as an adult, I learned that Jesus was anything but comfortable. Jesus made a habit of upsetting the settled order. And his message was a hard message, one that required people like me to make decisions about life and values and priorities that ran counter to society's values and priorities.

So the evidence about Jesus upset my expectation of a comfortable, non-threatening Christianity, every bit as much as the cure of the blind man confounded his neighbors. And that leads me to ask: just who is this man, anyway?

For professional reasons, I often try to stand in the shoes of my jurors, to see if they can help me reach my own verdict. In trying to answer the Jesus question, I, who am confused like the neighbors, have tried to put myself in the shoes of others: saints, theologians, anyone who can help me sort it out. I have even tried standing in the shoes of the Pharisees and the man born blind. And I find that each offers me some insight.

. . . . . .

From the Pharisees, I learn not to try to wedge Jesus into my preconceptions, because Jesus defies logic. The Pharisees drew an entirely logical inference from the evidence; it is a mistake for us to vilify them for doing so. But had they been correct, then this man Jesus, like so many false Messiahs, would have faded into history, remembered only by scholars of ancient Judaism. As we know, that did not happen. Instead, this itinerant preacher from an obscure corner of the world became the fulcrum of Western history; and his life and death are remembered and celebrated in every corner of the globe. There's nothing logical about that. But it's irrefutably true.

So logic will not provide the answer where Jesus is concerned. If I look at him through eyes that perceive only the things that are obvious, and that make sense by the world's lights, I will never see him.

And from the blind man? Well, originally I did not think the blind man had anything to teach me. After all, his was an easy faith: who in his position wouldn't believe that Jesus was the Son of Man? I, by contrast, have never had my own personal miracle to reinforce my beliefs.

Nonetheless, I've concluded that I can learn something from the man born blind. He was untroubled by logic, because what happened to him was not logical. And he was not confused, because he had been touched by a powerful encounter with the divine. As a result, from the very first moment, he was looking through eyes that saw beyond the logical: the eyes of faith. If I am to figure out who Jesus is, I must look through those eyes, too.

. . . . . .

Of course, you and I cannot look at Jesus and the world with such pristine eyes. Unlike the man born blind, we have already seen far too much. And logic tends to overwhelm the counter-intuitive message of Jesus in the eyes of those who see the world only for what it is.

But the cornerstone of the blind man's faith is that he never saw the world for what it was. And reasoning by analogy from the blind man's experience, the cornerstone of our faith must be the refusal to see the world only as it appears. We cannot hope to make sense of God, or squeeze his inscrutable agenda into the confines of our limited perspectives. But we can ask, humbly, prayerfully, that Jesus will touch our eyes, too, so that we can be open to the limitless possibility that is the vision of God. He has done so, in baptism and throughout our lives, and he will do it again. That, for me, is the message of this Gospel story.

They have Moses and the prophets; they should listen to them.
—Luke 16:29

I RECENTLY SENTENCED A YOUNG MAN to fifteen months in prison. A member of an insular Hasidic sect that lives in a small theocratic village northwest of New York City, he played a minor role in a massive fraud scheme involving members of his community. Pleading for the lowest possible sentence, his lawyer argued that the defendant was a fundamentally good person who had fallen under the influence of evil people because his father died when he was very young. "You cannot imagine how important the guidance of a father is in this community," the lawyer exhorted. "Of course, my client attended the yeshiva with the other boys, but ultimately the father is responsible for teaching his son, and this boy's father was dead."

I sympathized with the young man's situation, but I was not impressed with the argument. "No doubt he suffered a great loss when his father died," I reminded the lawyer, "but he went to school, and there he learned what his father knew, and his father's father, and his father's father's father before that. He learned Talmud and Mishnah, and above all he learned Torah, the law of Sinai, which says in no uncertain terms NO STEALING. He should have listened to Moses and the prophets. He did not, and today he pays the price."

The same phrase about Moses and the prophets came to mind when the World Trade Center evaporated. I was one of the lucky New Yorkers who was not directly affected by this monumental tragedy. But my Sunday school class expected me to make some sense out of it. They wanted to know why an omnipotent God did not step in and stop this from happening. Frankly, I wanted to know the same thing. So I thought about it for a long time.

And here is what I shared with my class: God has stepped in. He has already taken steps to prevent men from preying upon men. God has sent us repeated messages. He has told us, in no uncertain terms, everything we need to know to keep evil at bay. Put God first in your hearts. Cherish the law of love. Place others' needs ahead of your own. Choose life, not death. Honor the Creator by honoring all of creation.

God has stepped in. He has sent the message in many languages. Moses said it. Micah and Isaiah and Jeremiah said it. Jesus said it. Mohammed the Prophet, blessed be he, said it. The Buddha said it, and so does the Dalai Lama. They used different words and images; they spoke out of their own times and cultures. All of them lived in eras of grief and struggle and oppression. Yet they all were convinced that hatred and violence were antithetical to God's plan for his creation. In one way or another, they gave us pretty much the same message. All we have to do is listen, and take it to heart.

Unfortunately, we do not always listen. Even if we do, we are prone to distort the message in ways subtle and not so subtle. And when someone's distorted vision of God's eternal truth trips us up, we become angry at God. We want to know why— why bad things happen to good people, why people must suffer. Above all, we want to know why God doesn't do something to stop it. We forget that he already has.

· · · · · ·

When I find myself wondering why God doesn't step in, I am reminded of the story of the rich man and Lazarus. Such a simple fable—a man who had everything in this life, but failed to share it with those less fortunate, is condemned to eternal torment, while the poor beggar he ignored finds his way to paradise. The rich man, thinking at last of someone other than himself, begs Abraham to send someone down to earth to warn his brothers of the fate that awaits them. It's almost like a prequel to Dickens' *Christmas Carol*, with the rich man in the role of Jacob Marley, praying that his Scrooge-like relatives might have a personal revelation.

But Abraham says that there will be no more special revelations, no more burning bushes for humanity. The message has been sent; the signs are there for all to read. Ignore them at your peril, he chides. If you will not listen to the ones who have already been sent, there's no reason to believe you'll take the message to heart just because a new face shows up to repeat it—even if he makes a spectacular entrance.

I have long harbored a secret wish. I wish God would acknowledge that we humans aren't going to get it by listening to Moses and the prophets. I wish God would come down through the clouds, make another appearance—hopefully to all of humanity at once—and read us the riot act. I wish it when I read about starving babies and rampant disease, when I confront young men and women who have immolated themselves on the altar of false values, or when I read about random acts of violence. And I shake my fist toward the heavens and cry out, "God, you idiot, why don't you just come down here and set us all straight?"

. . . . . .

My wish is born of a certain despair. Nonetheless, I suppose it is a sign of God's loving patience with human beings that he doesn't grant it, but leaves us to figure the truth out for ourselves. Or, perhaps, it is a sign of hope. From the perspective of infinity, God may see a day when men and women everywhere will let the message of Moses and the Prophets drown out our personal gospels—when we will finally get it right. But today, with a gaping hole in the New York skyline and a young man wasting precious time in prison, I do not see that day. And I am tired of waiting for it.

Unless I wash your feet, you have no part of me.

—John 13:8

A FEW DAYS AGO I toured the Frozen Zone around Ground Zero in Lower Manhattan. A police chief who is working with me on a project made the arrangements. Another judge and I got the VIP treatment—hard hats with fancy decals, police escort to the viewing platform, senior mayoral aide driving us around The Hole in an official golf cart. The works.

I never felt less important in my life. Or less significant.

The images of Ground Zero in the hours and days after the attack are seared in the brain of every American. But by the mid-November day when I made my pilgrimage, only buildings four and six were still standing, and their charred wreckage was coming down. It was apparent that the site would be completely cleared by Christmas. From above, the gaping hole in the ground looked no different than the one at every other construction site before the new footings are poured—a familiar enough sight in New York City. There were construction workers everywhere—guys in their jeans and plaid shirts and heavy boots, tool belts on their waists, dirt on their faces. It was dusty, but so are all construction sites. Most telling, there were no longer a lot of emergency workers, police or firemen. In fact, it was pretty sanitized compared to a month earlier. Even the smell was not so smelly. Only the acrid aroma of memory distinguished the place from uptown blocks where tenements were coming down so skyscrapers could rise.

. . . . . .

No, it wasn't The Hole that conveyed the horror of what had happened. It was other things.

I was disoriented. I could not make sense of the Lower Manhattan grid. When the towers were standing, I could tell you where every street was, and how to get to every building in the area. But without the towers, familiar landmarks seemed to be in all the wrong places. Church Street (the continuation of Trinity Place, which runs behind Trinity Church) went the "wrong" way. Century 21, the department store, was not where I thought it should be. The new Millennium Hotel was shrouded in a cloth binding, like some sort of giant glass mummy. What had been Seven World Trade was already paved over with concrete.

Familiar buildings, seen up close, bore horrifying scars. It looked like Cookie Monster had taken a bite out of the southeast corner of the American Express Building in the World Financial Center. 130 Liberty Street, where my husband had his first job after business school—and where we spent a memorable Sunday afternoon stuck in an elevator—was charred and open to the elements. All the cleaning fluids of New York had not erased the grime from the black facade of One Liberty Plaza.

In a parking garage on Greenwich Street sat cars that had been carefully parked in the early morning hours of September 11, batteries dead. Hundreds of small businesses were shuttered. The brave pioneers who had opened for business looked to be pretty empty. I did not need newspapers to tell me about the bankruptcies to come, the ruins yet to be created.

. . . . . .

Across what was once the West Side Highway—now the world's largest staging area—Battery Park City was a shadow of its former bustling self. An occasional school bus traversed the Esplanade, designed to be a vehicle-free zone but now the only route taking residents out to the north. Returning apartment dwellers were outnumbered by the gawking tourists, whose presence was in many ways more disruptive than the background noise from heavy equipment. The black granite wall that memorializes every policeman killed in the line of duty in New York City—which just happens to be in Battery Park City—had been co-opted to serve as an impromptu memorial to the uniformed services personnel who died trying to save others. Photographs, flowers, letters and badges left by hundreds of police and fire units whose members came to help sat under a protective canopy in silent tribute.

Of course, as is always the case, in the midst of death there was life. Area residents, city workers and construction crews had become fast friends, and greeted each other by name and with a wave. Signs in bar windows made it clear that those who were thirsty would be given to drink. And Giovanni's Restaurant, buried on a side street where I couldn't believe anyone ever came, was festooned in little white lights. Everyone, in his own way, had made common cause against the terror. Everyone, in his own way, was part of a special band of brothers and sisters who would not admit defeat.

All this I saw from my little golf cart. I admired, and wept, and even said a word or two to God.

. . . . . .

As we turned up Albany Street on our way back to the car, we encountered two cheerful young women wearing bright yellow slickers. One was holding a hose. The other was waving passers-by onto a low plywood platform over the sidewalk. As Frozen Zone workers emerged—tired, dirty and hungry—from their long day's work, they dutifully stepped up, lifted their feet, and exposed the soles of their shoes to the hoses. A spritz, and their feet were clean. They hopped back down and vanished into the warmth and light of the Marriott Hotel across the street. There, the Red Cross offered food and fellowship to those who had seen the worst and yet kept coming back, day after day.

The two women running the foot washing station were delightful. They radiated warm welcomes. The blonde with the hose flashed a thousand megawatt smile, which she trained on everyone who passed. They saw nothing demeaning in what they were doing.

The woman directing traffic started to wave our little group up onto the platform. But our hard hats did not sufficiently disguise the fact that we were visitors. Before we could climb up, she said, "Are you going into the hotel?" When we answered no, she said, "Oh, then you can sail right through. You only need to wash your shoes if you're going in to eat."

She beamed as she waved us on. No doubt she thought she was doing us a favor. After all, dusk was falling and the wind had picked up. Who would want to walk the streets of Lower Manhattan in November wearing wet shoes?

. . . . . .

Our tour guide was certainly pleased that he could keep his feet dry. "They've just changed that rule," he told us. "Until a few days ago, everyone who left the site had to hose off their shoes." He sauntered past the platform and turned the corner toward his makeshift office. The rest of our party followed.

I hesitated. Like some anti-Peter, I wanted to say, "Please, won't you wash my feet?" I wanted to step up onto that platform and let the hose play over my shoes until they were soaked through. Then, properly cleansed, I wanted to go into the hotel and sit down at table with the people who had done things and seen things that no VIP tour could show me. I wanted that mark of belonging, to be part of what I was only visiting—something that was terrible and wonderful, that was bigger and sadder and holier than any endeavor in which I had ever participated. I longed to commune with the people who had participated in the cheerful women's simple and beautiful Maundy. I actually resented the fact that I would have gotten my feet washed if only I had come down a week sooner—before the rules changed.

The rest of my group would not have understood. Neither would the two cheerful young women. So I walked past the platform and turned the corner.

But when no one was looking, I jumped in a puddle formed by run-off from the hose.

. . . . . .

A man planted a vineyard, and leased it to tenants, and went to another country for a long time.

—Luke 20:9

I NEVER THOUGHT MUCH about the parable known as The Man Who Had a Vineyard until my rector asked me to preach a sermon about it. I soon realized that this was one troublesome tale. In fact, it's a really stupid story about really stupid people.

You have this landlord, who is not like any landlord I have ever seen. He has problem tenants who won't pay their rent. Does he serve them with an eviction notice? No. He sends three of his best people to collect the rent. Each poor fellow comes back more beaten and bruised than his predecessor. Does the landlord call upon the law for help? Certainly not. He dispatches his son and heir to the vineyard, on the theory that the tenants will respect the son. Why the landlord should think this is beyond me. After all, nothing the tenants have done so far could possibly give rise to such an inference.

But the tenants are equally dense. For reasons I cannot begin to fathom, they are under the impression that they can keep the landlord's property for themselves if only they get rid of the son. My (admittedly limited) research reveals no such principle in the law governing Roman-occupied Judea. Nonetheless, the tenants kill the son in order to retain the vineyard for themselves. It doesn't work, of course—once he loses his son, the landlord finally realizes the enormity of the threat to his interests and takes back his vineyard. At the story's end, he has his land. But he has no heir. In a Middle Eastern society of the first millennium, that is a really bad position in which to find yourself.

This parable doesn't make a whole lot of sense to the judge in me. But I finally found a way to think about The Man Who Had a Vineyard that made sense: as a story about power and authority, order and chaos.

It may not be immediately apparent what those things have to do with the parable of The Man Who Had a Vineyard. But, in my line of work, these are the kind of things you have occasion to ruminate about. After all, a judge is someone who has authority to enforce the law, which is society's bulwark for order and against chaos. I see power and authority, order and chaos in pretty much everything I do. Certainly, a fair number of the cases I hear have to do with abuses of power, and betrayals or even abdications of authority.

As a result, I have developed a theory about power and authority and how they work. My theory posits that the two concepts are related, but they aren't the same thing. Power is the ability to do something. It comes from the Latin root word *potere*, (to be able). Authority, on the other hand, is about having permission to do something. Indeed, the word derives from the Latin word *auctoritas*, which comes from an old agricultural term that implies "to act in a nurturing way." Here's the difference: the police have the power to arrest a citizen simply by virtue of their badges and guns, whether he has done anything wrong or not; but they only have the authority to arrest if there is probable cause to believe the citizen has committed a crime.

. . . . . .

My theory, which is quite simplistic and probably even self-evident, is that power and authority work best when they work together. Power gives effect to authority, while authority confers permission—sometimes called jurisdiction—to exercise power. Authority acts as a brake, a restraint, on power's sheer brute force. Authority is the civilizing force behind every exercise of power, legitimating it and rendering it socially and morally acceptable. And so, when power is exercised with authority, order ensues. By contrast, when power is not legitimated by authority, or when authority to exercise power is abdicated, the result is chaos.

The parable of The Man Who Had a Vineyard turns out to be a pretty good illustration of my theory. The landlord owns the vineyard. Ownership gives him authority over his patch of land. The landlord put tenants there to take care of it. They have no legal right to the vineyard beyond what the landlord has given them—they have no authority over it. Yet they are physically present on the vineyard, and the simple fact of possession gives them power—power that they exercise without authority, in violation of the landlord's right, by withholding his rents, by pummeling his servants and even by killing his son. The landlord does not have possession, so he does not have physical power over his property. Of course, the law is on his side, and he could invoke its power. But for a long time, the landlord refuses to do so. One party has authority without power, the other has power without authority. The two are not operating hand in hand. The result is chaos.

Finally, the landlord exercises the power that ownership confers on him and moves to take back his land. The tenants cannot confer authority over the land on

· · · · · ·

themselves, even by killing the son, so once the landlord moves against them—when power is exercised with the full backing of authority—they are, in the words of the Gospel, destroyed. Power and authority join forces, and order is restored.

You won't find this interpretation in any biblical commentary. Scholars and theologians usually take a literalist approach to this parable—God is the man, the prophets are the servants, Jesus is the murdered son, Israel (or God's special relationship with Israel) is the vineyard that is given to others. Then they argue over whether Jesus ever told this story at all, or whether it is an invention of the post-Resurrection community. I prefer to take the story on its own terms and to imagine that Jesus really did tell it. But it's hard to believe that Jesus would tell a story where God was so dumb.

My version of The Man Who Had a Vineyard does make sense, given what was happening to and around Jesus when he told the story. Holy Week, of which this story is an integral part, is all about power and authority, order and chaos.

It is important to remember when Jesus told this parable. It is the day after he has entered Jerusalem in triumph. He has gone to the Temple and smashed the tables of the moneychangers—tables that were under the direct supervision of the religious leadership. Then, in a very in-your-face gesture, he camps out on their turf, teaching and drawing crowds. Jesus is exercising power in the face of his enemies' authority, and as far as the Temple leaders are concerned, it is creating chaos.

Just before Jesus tells the parable, the chief priests, scribes and elders challenge him. "By whose authority are you doing these things?" they ask him, knowing full well that it's not by theirs. Jesus replies with the story of The Man Who Had a Vineyard.

· · · · · ·

Jesus knows that the Temple leaders feel threatened by his power to cure the sick, to free the possessed, and to draw crowds. And he knows that they also feel threatened by his teaching, which is so grounded in ultimate truth that people are saying, "He teaches as one with authority." Jesus has power and authority over demons, and disease, and even over the people. Because of that, the Temple leadership wants to kill him.

But Jesus knows something else. He knows that the Temple leaders do not have both power and authority over him. They have authority to judge him guilty of offenses against the Jewish religion. The Roman occupiers left the Jews this much local autonomy. At what passes for a trial before the Sanhedrin, blasphemy—a religious crime—will be the charge brought against Jesus.

However, theirs is an empty verdict. The Romans have eliminated the Sanhedrin's ability to impose the death sentence. So Jesus' enemies have no legal power to kill him. Of course they had the physical power to kill Jesus, in the same sense that the tenants had power over the vineyard. All it would have taken was an angry mob and a few stones. We know from reading other Gospel stories, like the one about the woman taken in adultery, that from time to time this mob power was exercised in Jesus' world. But Jesus was no harlot, to whom the Romans would be indifferent. He was a popular and charismatic figure, with a large following. The Temple leaders were afraid to deal with Jesus as they had dealt with the adulteress, because they feared that the people would rise up against them—a development that would not escape official notice. It was, in short, too dangerous for Jesus' enemies to take unauthorized action against him.

That is the backdrop against which Jesus tells the story of The Man Who Had a Vineyard—a story that his inquisitors immediately understood to be "a story against them." Jesus is sparring with his enemies, trying to figure out how they will get to him. If they listened carefully, they could hear him pointing out that they would only make trouble for themselves if they took action against him.

As the story of Jesus' last days plays out, this theme of power and authority continues. Look ahead a few days, to Luke's account of the Passion. The Temple leadership will think of a way around its lack of authority by enlisting the aid of the hated Romans. Only a few days after Jesus taunts their inability to do away with him legitimately, he will come face to face with Pilate, the Roman governor, a man who clearly has the authority to put Jesus to death.

But Pilate's authority also has its limits. It runs only to the civil law. Pilate has no jurisdiction over religious offenses against Judaism. He can crucify Jesus, but only for a crime against the good order of the Empire. Anything else would be an illegitimate exercise of power.

So the Temple leaders must recast Jesus' crime as one against Rome. And they will. They will claim that Jesus has perverted the nation by saying that he is a King—the ultimate offense in the eyes of a Roman. They try to fuse power and authority in one place, in one person, in Pilate, in a way that will result in Jesus' death—a very public, utterly humiliating death, one that will demoralize his followers and defuse the movement that is beginning to gather momentum in his wake. Then order will be restored—or so they imagine.

They are wrong. Power and authority will not fuse in the Roman governor. Pilate will find no basis for their civil accusations. He sees no evidence that Jesus has committed a crime against the Empire. Pilate does not find Jesus to be guilty of anything. Therefore, he has no authority to kill him. Power and authority can work together in this situation, but only if Pilate releases a man he believes to be innocent.

As we know, Pilate does not release the innocent man. Instead, he abdicates his authority to the mob. The words Luke uses are, "Pilate gave his verdict that their demand should be granted" (Lk 23:24). He does not say that Jesus is guilty—only that the mob should be appeased. Roman power is exercised without authority. Just as in the story of the man who had a vineyard, an innocent man is put to death.

At Jesus' death, chaos ensues. The sun's light fails, and the curtain that enshrouds the Holy of Holies is torn in two. Jesus' friends scatter and hide.

Then night falls, and all is quiet. For a moment, it seems that order is restored.

That, it turns out, is an illusion. Soon, it will become clear that the world has turned upside down. A tomb will be found empty. A dead man will show up in the room where his friends are cowering and ask for something to eat. Illiterate fishermen will begin to preach in tongues. A new kind of power—the power of love—will fuse with a new kind of authority, in a jurisdiction where the mighty are cast

. . . . . .

down and the humble and meek rule. And the stone that the builders rejected will become the cornerstone of a new social order—one in which an instrument of shame and torture becomes a symbol of triumph and hope. This is chaos indeed, and out of it will emerge a new creation. It is the chaos that will change the world.

> *When the man saw that he did not prevail against Jacob, he struck him on the hip socket; and Jacob's hip went out of joint as he wrestled with him.*
>
> —Genesis 32:25

HE CHEATED, YOU KNOW.

That "man"—God or angel or whatever—cheated when he administered that karate chop to Jacob's thigh.

Wrestling is the most ancient of sports, and the rules haven't changed much over the millennia. I checked them on the web. It was just as I suspected: striking one's opponent on the hip socket—or anywhere else, for that matter—is an illegal move. But once the heavenly opponent decided he wanted to win the world's most famous wrestling match, Jacob never had a chance.

Because, you see, God cheats.

That the God of the Bible cheats should come as no surprise to readers of Scripture. The divine saga is replete with instances of God's bending, if not breaking, the rules so that His Will Would Be Done. Post-menopausal women and virgins having babies. Frogs and locusts and rivers of blood. Waters parting. Stone walls crumbling at the trumpet's blast. Food for weeks from a day's worth of flour. Empty oil lamps burning for eight days. And then there's the biggest cheat of all—the triumphant cross, the empty tomb. Oh, God cheats, all right. He cheats big time.

. . . . . .

The questions this raises are three: Why does God want to cheat? Why does God need to cheat? And is this phenomenon restricted to ages past, or is God still cheating?

What is so important to God that it warrants cheating? Well, for whom does God cheat? Ah, yes—Jacob. Jacob always struck me as someone worthy of a kick in the pants, never mind a crack on the hip. Jacob was a liar, a cheat, a trickster, a cad, a coward, a thief and an ingrate. He was envious, arrogant and crafty. He played favorites. And he wanted things his way. Who else in the Bible responds to a vision of angels rushing up and down the stairway to paradise by saying, "*If* God will be with me, and will keep me in this way that I go, and will give me bread to eat and clothing to wear, so that I come again to my father's house in peace, then the Lord shall be my God" (Gen 28:20–21). He won't even take heaven if he can't have it on his own terms—and he got an advance peek! "God, if you will be nice to me, then I will be nice to you." What cheek! And how very familiar he seems. He sounds just like someone I know—someone I know very, very well.

Anyway, for utterly unfathomable reasons, it seems that God took a liking to this despicable creature and wanted to give him something. Something wonderful—a new name; a sign of divine favor. A blessing. But God, being God, has this thing about free will. The blessing is there for the taking, but God won't force it on you. In fact, if you want the blessing, you have to hang on to God for dear life and not let go. Only then can you have what God has always wanted to give.

That's why God, The Supreme Being Who Made All Things, had to cheat. You see, Jacob was not the sort of fellow who normally hung on to anyone or anything.

. . . . .

He was a primitive Master of the Universe. Jacob was strong. Jacob was self-suffi-cient. Jacob was in charge. Jacob had left his own people yet prospered mightily—four wives, thirteen healthy children, flocks that went on forever, untold riches. And he did it all without ever once asking God for help (it's true: read chapters 29, 30 and 31 of the Book of Genesis if you doubt me). Jacob was even capable of wrestling an angel to a draw. Cling to God? Hardly. Jacob was a walking piece of Cling-Free. How else was God to get past Jacob's defenses, to see if The Man Who Had Almost Everything wanted something infinitely more wonderful, except to cheat? There wasn't any other way.

Does God still cheat? Well, your major motion picture miracles are pretty much a thing of the past. But life is full of karate chops to the thigh, and from time to time we see that The Big Guy is still up to his old tricks. Think of the fellow who loses his job but finds instead the courage and freedom to do what he really loves. Or the bored wife whose extra-marital affair becomes the mirror through which she sees how wonderful her husband really is. Or the young person who reaches the end of the line—the line of coke, the line at the bar, the pick-up line that pre-cedes another meaningless sexual encounter—only to find the strength to search for something better, one day at a time. Think of all the awful, self-destructive choices we make that become, by God's grace, the vehicles of our transformation. All that life from all that death. Yes, God still cheats. Even though we are Jacob in every way, God thinks we are worth it—and he'll do whatever it takes to offer us the blessing, if only we can hang on.

. . . . . .

I wish I could say I see a lot of this sort of transformation in my line of work. I don't. God gives us the freedom to let go and end the wrestling match when we feel that blow to the hip socket, and most people exercise their human freedom very differently than Jacob did. In my experience, most criminals are only sorry they got caught, and most bad businessmen remain convinced in their heart of hearts that sharp practices pay, and most bigots are unshaken in their hatreds. I hear a lot of pieties, especially from people who are about to pay for their misdeeds, but all too often they ring hollow. I want to believe that something good will come out of a person's encounters with the law, but I've never put much stock in deathbed confessions.

And then something happens to pull me up short.

I have a letter in the top drawer of the credenza behind my desk. It's from a young man—I'll call him Larry—who was convicted of robbing a postal truck. Larry was a college student with good prospects—he wanted to work with kids—but he had a drug problem, and he hung out with a bad crowd. It all caught up with him when that postal truck crashed into a tree and catapulted him into the hands of the Postal Inspector. I hated to do it, but I gave him eighteen months in the joint—the minimum sentence, but enough to put quite a crimp in a young man's life. Many young men Larry's age have been hopelessly ruined by eighteen months behind bars. Nonetheless, I believed that the boot camp/shock incarceration facility where the Bureau of Prisons placed him was his last hope. I knew it was his last chance.

. . . . . .

About a year later, Larry sent me a letter from prison. I get them from time to time, and they're usually not pleasant reading. But Larry's was different. This is what he said:

> Your honor, I just wanted to write you expressing my gratitude for the opportunity (Life Learning Experience) you made possible by sending me to the I.C.C./Lewisburg, PA....This was truly an enlightening experience. Throughout this experience I have learned a lot about the tools (skills) one needs to be able to live life on a daily basis, honestly and respectfully to self and others (society)...The most essential tool is self-discipline...this program has allowed me the opportunity to live for 7 months, on a daily basis, under an intense routine, depending on my inner ability, and doing it without depending on drugs.

Larry's going to make it. He did not let go.

The story of Jacob's dysfunctional family ends with one of the most hopeful pronouncements in all of Scripture: "You meant it for ill, but God meant it for good... So have no fear: I myself will provide for you and your little ones" (Gen 50:20–21). Whenever I am tempted to forget that blessed truth, I pull out Larry's letter. Larry was up to no good when he tried to rob that mail truck, but God can work with pretty much anything we throw at him. He'll use whatever it takes to bring us to the point where the best we can do is grab hold and ask him for that blessing. We can count on it. So have no fear.

And remember: when he strikes you on the hip socket, don't let go. Hang on for dear life, and whatever you do, don't let go.

In a certain city there was a judge who neither feared God nor had respect for people. In that city there was a widow who kept coming to him and saying, "Grant me justice against my opponent." For a while he refused; but later he said to himself, "Though I have no fear of God and no respect for anyone, yet because this widow keeps bothering me, I will grant her justice, so that she may not wear me out by continually coming."

—Luke 18:2–5

THIS IS AN EASY PARABLE, right? Jesus gives us an entirely sympathetic character (the widow, always good for a tear) and an entirely unsympathetic character (the judge, who fears nothing and no one, and who, lest you not get it, is called "unjust"). The widow asks for justice, which is a loaded word if ever there was one. But since Luke starts the story by telling us what it means—"pray always and [don't] lose heart"—it seems clear that, for the widow, "justice" means winning her case. And that's what she gets in the end. She wins her case, simply by being a pest.

I find this a troubling story. For me, the judge behaves unjustly by giving in to the widow just so he can get rid of her. After all, who says that the widow ought to prevail in this particular dispute? We know nothing about the nature of her claim, or the defense that her opponent might offer.

But she asks for justice, you may say, and the judge gives her justice! Doesn't that suggest that she was in the right?

· · · · · ·

Maybe in a parable, but not on Gabbatha. In my experience, both sides in a case want justice. Unfortunately, they have radically different notions of what justice entails. So it undoubtedly was with the widow and her opponent. The judge is the professional dispenser of "justice"—not a litigant's personal vision of justice, but "justice" in the higher (which is to say, the legal) sense. It is his job to hear both sides of the case and then decide the issue based on objective and impartial principles. In the parable, the judge apparently decides the case without reference to the merits, just to be rid of it. As far as we know, he doesn't even give the other fellow a chance to tell his side of the story. That seems to me a strange sort of "justice."

I have trouble with this parable for another reason. The reader is not supposed to feel sorry for the "unjust" judge. But I have a great deal of sympathy for him, because I know just how he felt every time the widow showed up to press her case. Like every judge, I have several score of pesky "widows" hanging around on my docket, demanding their version of justice loudly and repeatedly. These people—most of whom are not actually widows, of course—are all absolutely convinced of the rightness of their cause. Some of them are indeed in the right, as I learn when I explore the facts. Others, however, are not. Quite a few of these "widows" are representing themselves—a few because they are poor or do not know how to find a lawyer, but most because they have been unable to convince a trained lawyer that their claims have sufficient merit to make the case worth taking. These "widows" tend to bombard a judge with lots of papers. Their papers tend to be hard to read. Often they are handwritten. Sometimes they are barely literate. And they always go on and on. This

. . . . . .

means the case takes a lot of time, whether it has merit or not. Many times the "widows" simply cannot or will not understand the rules of litigation, even though those rules apply to everyone including people who represent themselves. Some of these "widows" are unable to grasp the possibility that they might not be entitled to the redress they seek.

Some of these people are obsessed with their lawsuits—a few to the point of mental illness. And when the judge decides that justice does not lie with their cause, things can get complicated. Often, there are recriminations: complaints of judicial misconduct, lawsuits against the judge, even threats or real acts of violence. We have no choice but to take such things seriously: a few judges who did not are no longer among the living.

Few things are as hard for judges as self-represented litigants who are pressing their private visions of justice. I quite understand the temptation to get rid of them through any means, even by giving in to their demands. I have felt it myself. But I absolutely cannot give in to it. To do so would violate my oath of office, drawn from the Bible, in which I swore to "do equal justice to the poor and rich alike." I must be careful to give their cases the same consideration I give to everyone; I must neither dismiss their claims out of hand nor award them unmerited relief.

My professional reaction to this parable divorces it from its literary context. The widow, along with her friends the orphan and the stranger, are the traditional Biblical archetypes for those who have right but not might on their side. So we are meant to understand that the judge is in thrall to evil forces, while the widow is

· · · · · ·

pressing a valid claim—one she ought to win on the merits, and would, if the judge were a good and honest jurist.

The problem, of course, is that some modern readers tend to overextend the metaphor, or to forget that it is a metaphor. They equate "justice" in every case with the cause of the less powerful or less wealthy litigant, and would have "just" judges rely on sympathy for the weaker party rather than parse out the equities according to the law. But in the real world, that's not always the way it is. Civil justice—legal justice—is not always the same thing as justice in the religious sense.

Of course, no one is supposed to read a commentary on civil justice into the story of the unjust judge: Jesus tells his listeners that the story is about the power of praying to a just and loving God. Nonetheless, enough Christians take this story literally that I wish that Jesus had chosen a different metaphor. My job is hard enough without having to deal with folks who believe that God is on their side just because they are the little guy.

A voice is heard in Ramah, wailing and loud lamentation,
Rachel weeping for her children.

—Jeremiah 31:15

I HATE IT WHEN their mothers show up at the sentencing.

They almost always come. They wear their Sunday-go-to-meeting finery or their best jeans and sweatshirts. They arrive in fancy cars or they scrounge the bus fare. They sit with family and friends or they sit alone in an empty courtroom. But they come. Whether they attended the trial or not (and they rarely attend the trial), they come. They come because moms are supposed to be there at the bad times. And sentencing is the baddest time of all.

They are always in my line of sight, sitting out there, hunched over, tears streaming down their anxious faces. Or ramrod straight, fighting back the waves of emotion, enduring a pain next to which the pangs of labor are as nothing. They are in my face, looking at me, daring me not to feel their pain.

And I do feel their pain. I am a mother, too. More than once, I have been unable to hold back my own tears. But I am not crying for their children. I am crying for them.

There comes a moment when I ask their sons and daughters if they have anything to say to me before sentence. They always start by apologizing to me, like children apologizing to the principal when they are sent to his office. I stop them

. . . . . .

right away. "You don't owe me an apology," I say. "Apologize to that lovely woman sitting in the back of the room. Apologize to your mother. Turn around and look at her. Look at what you have done to her. How could you have done this to her?"

That is my moment of ultimate power. I may give them fifty years in jail, but it's not as cruel as forcing them to look at their grieving mothers. It can't be as hard for them to hear the words of judgment as it is to listen to the sobs swelling in the background just after sentence is pronounced. I know how much it hurts. I have watched hardened criminals, guilty of the most heinous crimes, wipe tears from their macho eyes at the sight and sound of their mothers weeping in the back of the room.

The mothers come for the same reason they came to the school play, or the baseball game, or the doctor's office. They come to offer support. A ministry of presence, as it were. Most times it does not help. People do not like being sentenced in front of their mothers. I can see it. There is a perceptible difference in the attitude of the ones whose mothers do not come. They do not lose their swagger. They do not tremble, or blink back tears. Mothers just make it go down harder. Yet they cannot stay away. The urge to be there is as strong as any countervailing consideration. Love is strong as death.

Sometimes these women send me letters, pleading for their sons and daughters. The lawyers tell them it might help. So they write to tell me about the Johnny or Susie who was a good child, who brought joy to their lives, who even now helps his mother. That is the person they want me to see. I, of course, cannot see that

. . . . . .

Johnny or Susie. I cannot see the babe at the breast, the child at play, the visitor who arrives with a kiss and a hug. I see their children through the lens of the evidence, and it is never a pretty picture. It is the evidence I am supposed to keep in mind as I sentence them. But with their mothers sitting there, I cannot demonize the men and women who stand before me. If I cannot see what their mothers see, I have to admit that, to these women, my defendants look very different from the criminals I have come to know. I have yet to hear from a mother who believed the worst about her child, no matter how awful that child may be. At some level, I find that comforting.

Because mothers almost always come to the sentencing, I just know Jesus' mother was at the Antonia on the cold Friday morning when Pilate's minions placed the Judgment Seat on Gabbatha. I know that the Passion narratives don't mention her presence, and that no self-respecting Jewess would have defiled herself by entering the governor's palace, especially on a high feast day. But that is of no moment. I am sure that she found a way to sneak in, to be as close to her son as she could get. Her face was veiled, but I know that her streaming eyes bore down on the Roman as he delivered, in a language she could not speak, words that no mother could fail to understand. I know this because I have been on the receiving end of that same despairing stare.

Could he see her hideously swollen eyes, hear her low moans? Did he sense her presence? Probably not. The Antonia was a large fortress, and there were guards aplenty to keep the hoi polloi at bay. Historians tell us that Pilate was a cruel and capricious bully, impervious even to his wife's importuning. And anyway, there was the question of the evidence. Pilate would have seen the Man in the light of the only evidence that mattered in an occupation zone: a restive mob outside his gate calling for blood, the local authorities unable to keep the peace and calling for help. No, the mother's tears would not have mattered.

The official witnesses, the Evangelists, did not see her. Their eyes did not fall on her small figure standing where no mother should have to be. But that does not mean she was not present, a sword rammed through her heart, just as old Simeon had predicted when she took her baby son to the temple so many years before.

I never used to see her, either. I saw only those whose presence was recorded in the book: the soldiers in their armor, the black-robed prelates with tzitzit flying, the governor clothed in purple and white. But not the mother, watching her son's sentencing. Not until I became a judge who is also a mother. Now I see her every time she walks into my courtroom. She is Rachel weeping for her children.

. . . . . .

> ### *What is truth?*
> —John 18:38

"REMEMBER, YOU ARE NOT PARTISANS," I tell my jurors just before they retire to deliberate. "Your job is to find the truth from the evidence."

Sometimes that is an easy task. But what happens when the truth is not readily apparent?

Case summary: A young man spoke up in a courtr_____moved. A struggle ensued between him a_____ed, no one seriousl_____spent seve_____d; the charg___

Th_____got involv_____ers for vio_____st-ed that_____ption of ongoing court proceed_____s, and they resented the accusation of racism and brut

> *So I held my tongue and said nothing; I refrained from rash words; but my pain became unbearable.*
>
> —Psalm 39

YOU MAY BE WONDERING about the previous page. Well, I wrote a piece on the text "What is truth" for inclusion in this book. It was a fabulous piece, if I do say so myself—one of the three or four best I did. My editor loved it. She thought it was a powerful meditation about something I observe every day—how Pilate was not really wrong, because truth is far from absolute in our imperfect world.

Unfortunately, we had to cut it. It had to go because it was about a case that is not yet over. I was moved—compelled, actually—to write "What is truth?" right after the jury delivered its verdict in a particularly sad and frustrating case. It was one of those cases where everyone loses and nobody feels good about the result—even though, as the jury saw things, it was the legally correct result. Now lawyers know that an appeal from a jury verdict in a case like this one—a "he said/she said" kind of case that turns on a jury's reconstruction of what really happened—is, frankly, a quixotic exercise. As a matter of fact, the lawyers who tried the case for the losing plaintiff refused to take it any further. But the plaintiff insists on pursuing the matter; he is certain that he will find vindication if only he persists. So, without anyone to help, he has appealed, and that appeal is wending its way through the Court of Appeals. Because the appellant is appearing without counsel, that journey

. . . . . .

is taking longer than usual. Until the Court of Appeals renders a decision, I cannot discuss the case in public—even in a piece that has nothing to do with the merits—without violating the Code of Judicial Conduct. So out of the manuscript it came.

Silence is part of the price I pay for having this job. And the silence is not just about pending cases. Where public matters are concerned, I can't talk about much of anything at all, at least not in any place resembling a public forum.

It's not that there isn't a lot to comment on. After all, the world is in crisis. Our country is at war against a stateless enemy dedicated to our destruction. A lively debate is raging about why we are in this pickle, and I have some pretty strong opinions on that subject. The institutional changes we are considering to cope with this mess could have profound implications for our national culture, and I have pretty strong opinions about some of those proposals, too. Furthermore, "America in Crisis" is not the only thing worth talking about. Genetic engineering, global warming, tax cuts, nuclear power, the end of "welfare as we know it," religious conflicts, conditions in migrant worker camps, the relationship between racial profiling and law enforcement—the list of topics on which I could write letters to the editor of the *New York Times* is endless.

And I do write them, but I can't send them. No judge can. It violates the Code of Judicial Conduct for judges to become involved in public debate over matters that might come before us and—far-fetched as it may seem—almost everything worth talking about is implicated in a lawsuit somewhere in this great land. Even issues that seem totally foreign to us, issues that touch on conditions in other lands, find their way into our courtrooms. Remember the brouhaha over a young African woman who feared genital mutilation? An American judge heard her asylum case. Almost anything can erupt into a lawsuit in one of our courtrooms, and the judges who preside in those courtrooms are supposed to be neutral arbiters of disputes. By expressing opinions on controversial matters, we might give the impression that we are not really neutral at all. Never mind that judges are generally well-informed citizens, and there isn't one of us who doesn't have our own opinions about these and hundreds of other subjects. And never mind that if some real blank slate ended up on the bench, society would balk at confiding important matters to such an ignoramus. It's a bit of a fiction, this "justice is blind" thing, but judges are nonetheless obligated to maintain it. So as a condition of taking the job, we agree to be very careful about what, and where, and when, we speak.

There is nothing about my job—not doing legal research, not writing opinions, not even sentencing criminals—that is as hard as keeping my mouth shut when I want to say something. I understand exactly what the Psalmist was saying—when you hear or read something that cries out for comment, it is really painful not to weigh in with my own views. Sometimes I just have to let it out—which explains the draft Op-Ed pieces that go straight from my word processor to the trash can, and the lively lunchtime disquisitions about the day's news that are heard only by my close friends and my confidential law clerks.

I did not think much about the implications of judicial silence before I went on the bench. When I first found myself muzzled, it was hard, if only because I had never been shy about expressing my opinions, loudly and forcefully. Keeping silent did not get any easier as time passed. And after a while, I began to wonder if civic silence were morally acceptable. I found it difficult to reconcile the ethical proscription against speaking out with the baptismal promises that requires me to "proclaim" the Good News, by word as well as by example. Jesus, who set the standard for us all, spoke out against injustice, hypocrisy and oppression. So did his most inspiring followers. The apostles, the martyrs ancient and modern, the saints of yesterday and today—all bore prophetic witness to the Good News. I believe that one of those prophets, Martin Luther King Jr., was on to something when he said, "Our lives begin to end the day that we become silent about things that matter." To be forced into silence about things that truly matter—against the remote possibility that I might someday have to address them from the bench—sometimes strikes me as a waste of the voice God has given me. It even makes me doubt my choice of vocation. Can I really use some man-made rule—one that does not even have the force of law—as an excuse to avoid an obligation of covenantal dimension?

It was a false issue. The real issue was whether I was misunderstanding my obligations as a Christian in order to justify something I had no business doing.

Nothing we do in life fails to exact a price. Committing your life to one partner means swearing off new and tempting attractions. Having a child means giving up some of the adult freedom we waited so long to attain. Higher education or vocational training means postponing financial independence. Going into public service means capping your income and downscaling your ambitions. Adopting religious observance means taking on obligations that your friends may neither understand nor appreciate. If you believe that you are called to do these or other things, you must be willing to pay the price in order to reap the rewards of your vocation.

I strongly believe that it is my vocation to be a judge at this time and in this place, that it is something I am called to do as part of my covenant life. If that is so, then it must be part of my baptismal obligation to limit my participation in civic discourse to writing opinions that draw their force from the rule of law rather than from my own preferences. The saints I am supposed to emulate are not the prophets, but the able, trustworthy, honest and God-fearing judges appointed by Moses to sit as judges over Israel (Ex 18:21). These fellows had a job to do—settling disputes among the people—and we know from reading the Torah that they did it. Indeed, that is all we know about them. They were honest, God-fearing men who did the work that was given them to do. In doing their job, they resisted evil, strove for justice and respected the dignity of those who came to them for help—all of which is enshrined in the baptismal covenant. But you can search the Scriptures until your eyes fall out, and you will never learn a thing about their politics, or their views on the issues of the day. If it was not necessary for them to make a public record of such things, then it could not possibly be necessary for me to do so.

Hardest of all for any judge is to be silent in the face of attacks. This was not always a problem; until quite recently no one would have thought of criticizing a judge for rendering a decision, even an unpopular one. It is only in the last couple of decades, as the process of judge-making has become more and more politicized, that judges have become fair game for attack by the press, politicians, pundits, and pretty much anyone else who cares to take a punch. And we cannot punch back. Our work—the opinions we write, the decisions we make, the verdicts we render—is supposed to speak for us. But since the accusations leveled against us are generally the product of someone's dissatisfaction with that very work, our opinions do not afford us much of a defense. Fortunately, I have not yet been publicly pilloried, but I have sat—mute, of course—while a dear friend who happens to be a very good judge endured the most vicious accusations of stupidity, and even cupidity, after handing down a difficult (and intellectually defensible) decision in a high profile case. I know my day is coming.

But judges are not the first public figures who have had to stand silent in the face of unfair charges. Long ago, a public man stood alone before the Judgment Seat and said nothing at all to answer his accusers. His work, too, was all that spoke for him. He had caused the blind to see and the lame to run and the crowds to draw closer to the Center of the Universe. And because that made his accusers crazy with jealousy and loathing, it afforded him no defense at all. Still, he remained silent—even when the person who held the power of life and death begged him to say something, anything, that might turn the tide in his favor.

Did he want to speak? Was his enforced silence painful, like the Psalmist's? Was his heart burning hot within him? Probably. I don't buy all that meek and mild stuff. After all, this Jesus, who spoke so eloquently for so long, had bested these same accusers in pointed debate time and again. He knew he could beat them this time as well, and before a larger and more important audience than he had ever commanded. I'll bet he wanted to answer the charges. He had to put a muzzle on his mouth at the last, and the pain of staying silent was probably harder to bear than the lash and the thorn.

But Jesus knew that there was something vocational in his silence, something holy and infinitely more eloquent than any words he might have uttered. "Who am I? I am what you saw and heard when I was walking freely among you," the silence said. "What more can I possibly say for myself?"

Jesus, of course, paid a terrible price for living out his vocational silence. He was tortured and killed in the most hideous way the men of his era could devise. The price of living out my vocational silence is hardly comparable. Right now, all I have to do is give up the satisfaction of publishing one of my creations, of which I am perhaps too proud. But even that small sacrifice hurts. When I realized I had to cut "What is truth?" I about threw a hissy fit. What that says about me I prefer not to contemplate.

. . . . . .

Then the father said to him, "Son, you are always with me, and all that I have is yours."

—Luke 15:31

YESTERDAY'S PAPER carried a story about a conference on Restorative Justice at a local law school. The Restorative Justice movement holds that punishment is a poor response to crime, and that a better model—better for the criminal, the victim and society—would focus on finding "meaningful" ways for offenders to make amends.

I can't claim to know much about the Restorative Justice movement, although some legal scholars and ethicists see it as a serious alternative to a criminal justice system based on Retributive Justice. I do not think that having criminals make amends to their victims is a bad thing—quite the contrary. Nonetheless, there were some "anti-punishment" comments in the article that rubbed me the wrong way. I guess that's because I am in the Retributive Justice business—the business of meting out punishment to admitted or convicted wrongdoers. And I don't think there's anything either wrong or un-Christian about what I do.

I reacted to the newspaper story in much the same way I react to many of the letters of support that deluge me as I prepare to sentence a convicted criminal. More often than not, the writers beg me to "do justice" by declining to punish the offender. They ask me to forgive him on society's behalf and wipe his slate clean. Often they cite Scripture in an effort to justify their request. Clergy are particularly likely to send such missives.

These letters set my teeth on edge. I think my correspondents, like some of the people in the Restorative Justice movement, tend to oversimplify concepts like justice and forgiveness, and in the process rob them of their moral force. They would have me clothe Retributive Justice in the mantle of what Dietrich Bonhoeffer called "cheap grace"—to conclude that punishment is misguided, because it suggests that we can earn forgiveness.

Baloney.

That actions have consequences is the most powerful moral lesson we learn as children. Teacher may forgive me for cheating on a test, but I get a zero anyway. Mom may forgive me for breaking the lamp, but I was told not to throw balls in the living room, so I'm still grounded. Dad may forgive me for wrecking his car, but his pardon does not erase the body damage, the rise in insurance rates, or the summons to Traffic Court. Fortunately, teacher and Mom and Dad continue to care about me despite my misbehavior, and want to help me as I deal with the inevitable fallout. That is one of life's great blessings. But they would be doing me no favors if they eliminated that nasty fallout. Consequences are a civilizing force. Without them, we would never learn proper behavior.

Punishment is the consequence of crime, and it is in no way inconsistent with forgiveness. Every single person who comes before me for sentencing apologizes. I tell them all the same thing: you owe me no apology. What I am really saying is this: you cannot expiate your crime by telling me that you are sorry. I am here to explain to you the consequences of your misbehavior. I would not be doing my job if I excused you from those consequences just because you are sorry.

In the same newspaper that ran the story on the Restorative Justice conference, there were at least a half dozen articles about various aspects of the Roman Catholic Church's current pedophilia scandal, which had just become public. In those earliest days, as the scandal began to surface, many people's reactions were perfumed with the scent of cheap grace. I remember particularly one cardinal's observation that swift and sure punishment for sexual misconduct might conflict with Jesus' mandate that we forgive each others' sins. But how could it? Sexual misconduct is both criminal under the civil law and sinful under God's. God will surely forgive the sin, but it does no violence to the concept of forgiveness to punish the crime. It perverts justice and accountability to do otherwise.

The whole pedophilic priest scandal has brought back a flood of unhappy memories about this forgiveness/punishment thing. Ten years ago, when I was Vice Chancellor of the Episcopal Diocese of New York, a newspaper contacted the bishop. It was planning to run a story about one of our priests, who had allegedly abused a young boy. Unable to obtain legal redress because the case was too old, the victim—now a grown man—had gone to the press. The phone call came just as we were putting the finishing touches on procedures for dealing with allegations of sexual misconduct by clergy. They called for swift investigation, punishment and pastoral response. Although the diocese had not yet formally adopted these recommendations, we decided to follow them as we dealt with this case. Within a week, the priest had admitted his behavior and renounced orders; the victim received an apology; and the priest's parish was told of the tragedy in as pastoral a way as possible. There was no "closure" and the whole affair inflicted a great deal of pain on innocent people, but we did what we thought was necessary so that the long process of dealing and healing could begin.

Brother, did we take a lot of heat. Mostly, our critics accused us of worrying more about the church's institutional liability than about offering Christian forgiveness to a repentant offender. Well, that was just plain wrong. He was offered forgiveness— also pastoral assistance and counseling to help him deal with the wrenching change in his life. What he was not offered was the opportunity to continue in priestly ministry. That would have been cheap grace. While this man's seriously sinful, scandalously harmful behavior could be forgiven, there was too much collateral damage—to his victims, his parish, his community, and, yes, to the institutional church—to gloss over the sin in the guise of loving the sinner. At the time, many perceived our response as the antithesis of pastoral. It hurt to have our bona fides questioned. A decade later, the public perception of child abuse in the church has undergone a radical change. I suspect that if our actions of a decade ago were to be judged by today's audience, we would come off looking pretty good.

The people who try to influence me at sentencing, the folks who thought my diocese was persecuting a poor benighted cleric, the first (but thankfully not the last) response of the Roman Catholic Church to the unfolding scandal—the common thread is that all see some inconsistency between forgiveness and consequences. But there is none. Jesus may have saved us from our sins, but he never said we didn't have to do penance for them. Jesus understood that actions have consequences, and he never minimized them.

As proof, my seventh and eighth grade Sunday school class would call your attention to the story of the Prodigal Son. They would not focus on the familiar details about the father's forgiveness: the robe and the ring and the fatted calf. No, they would point to the oft-overlooked end of the parable. When the good son complains about the reception accorded his ne'er-do-well brother, the father chides him, "Son, you are always with me, and all that I have is yours." Think about what he is saying. The father does not pretend that things will go back to the way they were just because he has killed the fatted calf. The younger son is welcome at home, but he will not resume his place as co-heir. That is his punishment. He has used up his inheritance and he must live with the consequences: dependence on his father's love and his brother's mercy for as long as he chooses to stay in their home, making his own way without prospects if he wants to be his own man. The boy's misbehavior did not destroy his father's love, and he can call on that love as he adjusts to the new realities of his life. But there is no cheap grace for the Prodigal Son: Justice for him is both restorative and retributive.

Call me old fashioned, but I think that's the way it should be.

. . . . . .

And should I not be concerned about Nineveh, that great city, in which there are more than a hundred and twenty thousand persons who do not know their right hand from their left, and also many animals?

—Jonah 4:11

YOU NEVER CAN TELL what will deflect the wrath of the judge.

Jonah wants the Ninevites punished for their wickedness. They are so bad, and Jonah is so horrified by their behavior, that he resists God's commission to warn them of impending doom. He resists because he is afraid that these evil people will find a way around what they deserve. And so they do. They repent. And God changes his mind about bringing calamity upon them.

That's what the Bible says. Me, I suspect that God's line about repentance is just a cover. I think the Lord stayed his hand because he went all soft and mushy over those helpless animals.

I say this because I have been turned from my "wrath" at the last minute any number of times, and it's almost always someone's helplessness that does the trick.

When I asked my senior law clerk to remind me of an example, he said, "Lorna Muldoon." I remember her well. Arrested for drug dealing, she knew the futility of going to trial because she'd been down this road before—many times. So she pled guilty, even though the Sentencing Guidelines mandated that she spend at least three years in federal prison. Her lawyer sent me a letter asking that I grant her a downward departure, and so did her minister and the director of the drug program into which she had belatedly checked herself. I was unmoved. Lorna had been given a lot of chances to turn her life around. I was suspicious of her "conversion." Time for her to pay the piper.

When I walked into the courtroom, however, I learned that she had been accepted into a unique drug treatment program that would take, not just Lorna, but her young daughter. And it hit me—if Lorna went to jail, her daughter was going to foster care. There was no one else to care for her. Lorna didn't know her right hand from her left, but the child was one of the "many animals" who would suffer if her mother received a richly deserved punishment. I couldn't bring myself to impose that collateral damage. So I granted the downward departure motion and sent Lorna to rehab. I certainly didn't do that because Lorna "repented." When I hear a defendant apologize, I can't help but suspect that he is mostly sorry he got caught. You can get cynical that way in my line of work—especially after a few of those apologetic defendants come back before you on a parole violation. I'll bet Jonah was suspicious of the "repentance" of the Ninevites, coming as it did in the shadow of calamity. I certainly would have been.

I don't have an omniscient God's ability to read people's hearts, so I can't tell if the repentance that's on display in my courtroom on judgment day is for real. But I am not immune to the plight of the weak and helpless. And it won the day at Lorna's sentencing.

. . . . . .

The people who want to take sentencing discretion away from judges are like Jonah. They are outraged over crime, and rightly so. They want criminals to suffer, and they don't want some neutral magistrate diluting the pain. They make their righteous indignation felt in their demands for mandatory minimum sentences, three-strikes-and-you're-out laws, and inflexible guidelines devised by panels applying the latest in penological theory. I understand exactly where they are coming from, and part of me sympathizes.

But God, apparently, is not a theorist. And we know from reading Jonah that he couldn't care less about the indignation of the righteous. There is no end to his mercy when it will affect the helpless. I can't always place the interests of the affected family and friends ahead of the demands of civil justice. Most times it would be downright inappropriate, no matter how great the pain. But sometimes, sparing Nineveh to save the animals strikes me as the right thing to do.

· · · · · ·

Take off your shoes from your feet, for the place on which you are standing is holy ground.

—Exodus 3:5

WHEN I WAS A CHILD, I almost always had to wear my shoes. Going barefoot violated the house rules. Too many things could go wrong, said my mother. Poison ivy. Bee stings. Cuts from hidden stones. Blisters from burning pavement.

So it was always a treat when I had permission to take off my shoes. And there were places where it was allowed. The swimming pool. The dance studio. The shore of Lake Erie. As I think back on my early years, I recognize these as some of the places where I was most joyful, most carefree, most myself. Most in tune with the universe. They were a child's holy ground.

I have put off the things of a child, but even now, the holiest of my holies are places where I can take off my shoes. The bedroom I share with my husband. The beach at Martha's Vineyard. The soft green grass in the park. The tiny rooms where I submit my tired muscles to a massage or a steam bath. These are places I associate with life's greatest pleasures. Flying kites and digging sand castles. Picnics. Relaxation. Trysting with my lover. Being tucked in at night.

It seems that, when I take off the shoes from my feet, quite by accident I come closest to God.

• • •

"Take off your shoes from your feet, for the place on which you are standing is holy ground."

I don't suppose many people associate this particular divine directive with the law. But I do.

When I was looking for a job at a New York City law firm, the strangest things pushed me away from one place and toward another. I turned down an offer from one outstanding firm because the tile on the floor reminded me of a dentist's office. Another reject was sepulchrally quiet and looked an awful lot like the set for Mr. Potter's bank in *It's a Wonderful Life*.

And the place I chose? Well, it was noisy, and people always seemed to be moving around. As I watched the activity from a couch in the main lobby—before I embarked on a single interview—I felt comfortable. I remember thinking to myself, "You could take off your shoes here." Which I did, many times, in the twenty years that followed. Night after night you could find me padding down those halls in my stocking feet, singing (not too loudly), on my way to the library or to a conference room, where the best lawyers I will ever know tried to make the law work for troubled clients.

I learned a lot about holiness in that place. When people come to lawyers, they are in trouble. Sometimes they are frightened. Other times they are angry. Often they are confused. They need someone to serve as their advocate within the system. They need someone to mediate their disputes, and if mediation fails, to intercede on their behalf at the bar of justice. Americans subscribe to the proposition that every person, no matter what he has done or how bad he may be, is entitled to such an advocate, mediator and intercessor when he comes face to face with The Law in all its majesty and terror.

Many people deride lawyers as slick mouthpieces who twist the law to serve unsavory and undeserving interests. This is not a new phenomenon; the Evangelists put nothing but contempt for lawyers (scribes) in Jesus' mouth. Yet when I use the words advocate and mediator and intercessor, I am reminded of the Litany of the Blessed Virgin Mary. The Mother of God has long worn the titles Advocatrix and Mediatrix, and we beg her regularly to "pray for us sinners"—to intercede on behalf of humanity in the Highest Court of All. It is an honor and a privilege to serve her function on earth. To do it well and honorably is a holy thing.

I did a lot of recruiting for my firm during the two decades I worked there. Whenever young law students asked me what had drawn me to that place, I replied: "It was noisy and I could walk down the hall barefoot." I'm sure that more than a few of them were shocked. But some weren't, and it was invariably they who accepted our job offers. They were the ones who heard what was in the deepest recesses of my heart: "Because it was holy ground."

• • •

"Take off your shoes from your feet, for the place on which you are standing is holy ground."

Courtrooms look a lot like churches when you walk in. There's that center aisle. The benches in the spectator section appear suspiciously like pews, and the railing that marks off the well separates the holy of holies from the hoi polloi as effectively as any rood screen. The jury box, off to one side, serves as the choir stalls for the vox populi. Front and center you find the bench, standing there like an altar or bimah—the repository of the law.

I don't think the similarities are coincidental. In Western culture, the law is a holy thing. It is the sacred centerpiece of the Judaeo-Christian story. God wove the law into the fabric of creation. He handed the fundamentals to Moses on the mountaintop. The essence of Israel's covenant with its deity was obedience to the rules inscribed on those stone tablets. Priests were the first legislators, and, as mediators between the human and the divine, they expanded the Decalogue into a code that governed a nation's temporal affairs. While the covenant was fresh in Israel's collective memory, the only earthly authority its people would accept were judges who applied God's law to resolve human conflicts. Jesus, the rabbi who taught with authority, came not to abolish the law, but to perfect it.

Sometimes I think it's too bad that the people who come to court don't shed their shoes at the courtroom door, just to remind them that they are all engaged in holy work. Lawyers guide their clients through the intricate ritual of dispute resolution that we as a people have chosen in preference to anarchy. Witnesses swear to be truth tellers, which, as Walter Brueggemann reminds us in his essays on law and covenant, is the cornerstone of the neighborhood we call society. Jurors listen carefully, then apply the law, together with a dose of common sense, to resolve the problems of others so that all may live in peace. And I—well, it's an imperfect analogy, but there's something about charging a jury that occasionally calls to mind a deity's handing two stone tablets, duly inscribed, to a waiting world.

At the end of each day's session, the judge is supposed to make a dramatic exit from the courtroom. Everyone rises, out of respect for my office, so I can descend from the bench and disappear into my chambers. For all my love of ritual, I am not very good at it. Lawyers and litigants stand puzzled, waiting for me to leave. As often as not, I am fumbling for the shoes I kicked off hours earlier. My bare feet are a reminder. The work that I am doing is God's work. The place on which I am standing is holy ground.

Gather the wheat into my barn, but the weeds you shall burn with unquenchable fire.

—Matthew 3:12

WHEN PEOPLE THINK about judges, they tend to think of a hanging judge, who punishes the wicked and avenges the wrongs done to innocent people. There are truly wicked people in this world, and if society is fortunate, they catch the attention of law enforcement and are brought to court for justice. When this sort finds their way into my courtroom, burning them with unquenchable fire is not far from my mind. That, however, is a dangerous feeling for any mere mortal to entertain.

The baddest dude I ever encountered was not the gang murderer, or the gunrunner, or even the s.o.b. who sweet-talked hundreds of hard-working middle class people into investing their life's savings in a get-rich-quick scheme. He was a fellow I will call Isaac Black. Isaac was a small-time hustler, a pimp, a drug dealer, and a thug, who terrorized a small housing project in Manhattan. He was a large man, and he enhanced his size by wearing steel-toed boots and beating the bejezus out of anyone smaller who got in his way. He took what he wanted when and where he wanted it. This included taking women into his wife's bed, to the everlasting confusion of his children.

Among the detritus he left in his wake was a young girl named Katie, who was so warped by her dependence on him—for drugs, for sex, for validation—that she "loved" him even when he grabbed her by the hair and held her face over an open gas flame until she submitted to his sadistic whims. During his trial for that assault, I came to hate Isaac with the perfect hatred the author of Psalm 139 reserved for those who hate the Lord. He was a noxious weed; unquenchable fire was far too good for him.

Lucky for him the law stayed my hand. When all was said and done, I could only give him fourteen years. I genuinely regretted that I could not put him away for longer, but the legislature decreed no greater sentence for the crime of assault. It was, however, a pleasure to sentence him to the maximum. I enjoyed every minute of it.

Afterward, I wondered at myself. Isaac was a sociopath, and I know that society—especially its weaker and more vulnerable members—needed someone like me to protect them from his twistedness. But what base impulse let me feel joy about sentencing a man to fourteen years in a place where he was unlikely to become a better person?

Nothing in the Bible suggests that God enjoys punishing his people for their transgressions. Indeed, the God of Israel had a tough time bringing himself to the point where he could punish Israel for breaking the covenant. God could not stop loving his people, even when they screwed up, so he kept giving them second chances. And when they finally forced his hand, he promised redemption: "For the days are surely coming, says the Lord, when I will restore the fortunes of my people, Israel and Judah...and I will bring them back to the land that I gave their

· · · · · ·

ancestors and they shall take possession of it" (Jer 30:3). Apparently, the old saw that goes "This hurts me more than it hurts you" is valid, at least in the context of loving punishment. Ask any parent. Administering much-needed discipline to an errant child is an act of love, but I would rather walk a bed of nails than ground my teenager on the eve of a big event. Should I not shed a tear when I ground someone else's child by putting him in jail?

If I am living out my baptismal vows faithfully, it should pain me to do what I have to do to the Isaac Blacks who come before me. That it sometimes does not only shows how far I am from loving my neighbor as myself—and how very unlike God I can be when I sit on the judgment seat.

> *Oh God, you declare your almighty power chiefly in*
> *showing mercy and pity....*
>
> —Collect, Proper 21, Book of Common Prayer

MARGIE ORPHY WAS a drug dealer, pure and simple. She was part of a small-time operation in a small town, but small-time drug operations can ruin many lives— lives of addicts and of the people who love them or depend on them. That is why the government targets them so aggressively. Last year, it targeted Margie's operation, and she found herself in my courtroom, charged with a crime that carried a mandatory minimum sentence of five years in a federal penitentiary.

By the time I met Margie, five years was tantamount to a life sentence. The woman who confronted me was shrunken, bloated and balding, with bleary eyes and tears running down her face. I thought she was about seventy years old. She was in fact between forty and fifty. An aggressive cancer had eaten away her youth and was now chowing down on life itself; it was questionable whether this woman would live for five months, forget about five years. When I viewed the videotapes that conclusively proved her a criminal, I saw no connection between the tall, vibrant, ribald woman on the screen and the pathetic creature who could barely hold her head up in court, who still smoked crack whenever she could find it because nothing else eased the killing pain.

. . . . . .

One of the frustrations of being a federal judge is that I don't have unfettered discretion to sentence as I would like. Congress sets the maximum sentence, and sometimes the minimum, and within those parameters a Sentencing Commission calculates guideline ranges that effectively tie a judge's hands once the prosecutor decides what crime to charge. These ranges give us very little discretion; the low end is rarely more than six to twelve months less than the high end. Occasionally we are able to "depart" from the guidelines, but not for all the reasons you might think. We are forbidden, for example, to consider the hardship that a prison sentence would work on a defendant's family, or whether an unhappy childhood contributed to his propensity to commit the crime. All in all, we have precious little wiggle room.

God, of course, is not in my position. When the Lord adjudicates, he has all the wiggle room he wants, and he does not hesitate to use it. He has been known to bargain with humankind ("Lord, if I can find fifty righteous men in Sodom...." Gen 18:24) and to be persuaded from taking out his full wrath on us ("Make a poisonous serpent, and set it on a pole; and everyone who is bitten shall look at it and live..." Num 21:9). We have gotten around his judgments by appealing to his pride ("Why should the Egyptians say, 'It was with evil intent that he brought them out to kill them in the mountains, and to consume them from the face of the earth?'" Ex 32:12) and by throwing ourselves on his mercy ("David said to Nathan, 'I have sinned against the Lord.' Nathan said to David, 'Now the Lord has put away your sin: you shall not die.'" Sam 12:13). Sometimes he simply talks himself out of carrying out his promised sentence. (Remember Jonah?) And some-

· · · · · ·

times, he administers the punishment but promises to make it all better, as when he exiled Judea but promised to destroy the agents of his own wrath. ("I am going to punish the king of Babylon and his land, as I punished the king of Assyria" Jer 50:18). Only his original promise to make us pay for the consequences of our misdeed ties his hands, and that not very tightly. One suspects that if God had not explicitly promised to punish us for our transgressions, he never would. Whatever the vision of the Book of Revelation, I expect he will make some last-minute adjustments to that final separation of the sheep from the goats.

I would like to have this breadth of discretion to deal with criminals as the spirit, or the moment, or the transgressor, moves me. Unfortunately, I do not have the ability to set aside the rules. But sometimes I can find ways around them.

No way was I sending Margie to die in jail. Once her doctors advised me that Margie had less than a year to live, I set the date for sentencing as far in the future as I could, and then made it clear to the Government that she would be getting time served. The prosecutor could take an appeal, of course, but by the time it was heard and decided, Margie would have gone to that Big Courtroom in the Sky.

Fortunately, I was working with a humane and reasonable prosecutor, and she knew a thing or two about getting around the rules as well. She arranged a proffer session at which Margie could give agents any information she had about drug dealing in her town. It turned out that Margie didn't know very much about the local drug dealers, but the prosecutor advised me that Margie had cooperated to an extent that would permit me to depart from the guideline range. To give me some

. . . . . .

more cushion, the government took no position on the sentence, giving me a signal that there would be no appeal.

And so, with a wink and a nod, I sentenced Margie to a term of supervised release, and we sent her home to die.

. . . . . .

> *...through him who shall come to be our Judge....*
> —Collect for the Courts of Justice, Book of Common Prayer

MOST PEOPLE HAVE AN IMAGE of a judge—derived from the Bible, burnished by TV and movies—as a dispenser of justice, just like the Lord God on the Last Day. That image is deeply rooted in our culture, and it's pretty terrific to be thought of in that way. But it is a gross exaggeration, especially since most of my work is civil rather than criminal in nature. Sorting out who is liable to whom in automobile accidents, recovering pension contributions from defaulting employers, or deciding if a corporation should have revealed more about its financial condition than was included in the annual report—well, it's very important to the people who are directly affected, but it does not have that Last Day feel to it. Often, it doesn't even seem to have a moral dimension.

But occasionally it happens that a civil lawsuit is not just a lawsuit. When that happens, when I really get to Dispense Justice, I come as close as it's possible to come to Sitting on the Throne Judging Right. And it is a powerful, soul-searing experience.

In my first year on the federal bench, I was handed an emergency application from a Chinese woman—I'll call her Annie—who ran a restaurant in a suburban community north of the courthouse. For twenty years, she had served Chinese food, mostly take-out, to the working class community in which she lived. Her

· · · · · ·

105

restaurant was little bigger than a storefront, but it had kept Annie independent after her husband walked out and enabled her to put a daughter through college. The business meant everything to Annie.

As the area around her restaurant gentrified, Annie began to lose customers to a fancier, eat-in Chinese restaurant down the street. But she was a canny business-woman. She began to cater to a new clientele: Mexican immigrants, most of them illegal, who gathered at the corner every morning, seeking work as day laborers. Annie, herself an immigrant, knew they had to eat, and she modified her menu to offer them familiar food. Soon they were her best customers.

They were also the subject of the ire of the community. Some of that anger was justified: the newcomers lived life in their own way, which clashed with the sensi-bilities of an All-American middle-class small town. Some of that anger was really fear: it had to do with property values and the thought of losing a hard-won invest-ment in a small piece of the American dream. Some of that anger was racism, pure and simple. Like so many things, the rights and wrongs were not always clear-cut. But the illegal immigrant question was a political hot potato in the town, and efforts to clean things up (read: clear the Mexicans out) had already spawned a number of lawsuits.

Annie rented her premises. She had always been a good tenant. In fact, her land-lord had promised to send a renewal lease in the mail. An eviction notice arrived instead. When she called to find out why, she was told that her restaurant was cre-ating problems in the neighborhood—loud noise, fighting, increased police calls, customers leaving trash in their wake, even fouling the street. All this was supposedly interfering with the ability of neighboring businesses to keep their customers and creating a public nuisance. The landlord planned to rent to a less controversial tenant, who would not be in the take-out food business.

Annie sued her landlord, and the case was assigned to me. At first I was mystified: landlord-tenant disputes are quintessentially state court matters, and private landlords like Annie's generally have no obligation to offer a tenant a renewal lease. But Annie insisted that she was being run out of town because she did business with the Mexicans. At a preliminary hearing, she presented evidence that the mayor and other town officials had persuaded the landlord not to renew her lease. If Annie could prove that the town officials were motivated by racism, not by economics or the "public nuisance" her restaurant was supposedly creating, she would be entitled to damages and an injunction that would allow her to stay in her long-time location.

I listened to the testimony about the deleterious effect that Annie's business was having on the neighborhood. The antiques dealer next door insisted things were so rowdy that he had to move to a new location. The owner of the Irish pub across the street complained about finding broken glass on the sidewalk and vomit in the gutter every morning. The police chief came armed with "statistics" showing an increase in police calls to Annie's restaurant. The real estate agent arrived with stories about how difficult it was to collect enough rent from a business as small as Annie's. And the mayor insisted that antipathy toward the Mexicans in the community had nothing to do with his "suggestion" to the landlord that Annie's business made trouble for the town.

After listening to them for two days, however, I concluded that they were dissembling. As the prophet Daniel said, their own mouths condemned them. For example, the landlord insisted that he decided not to renew Annie's lease because he didn't want to have a restaurant in his premises. But the real estate agent who was trying to re-rent the property showed it to several restaurateurs. One of them actually made an offer for the space; the landlord rejected it, but only because the rent offered was too low. One neighboring tenant who was offended by Annie's clientele complained that the sidewalks were never fouled until Annie changed her menu. But another admitted that there had been similar problems for many years before the day laborers arrived. And what were the odds that the sidewalk residue associated with drunken patrons was the product of a tiny restaurant that closed every night by 10 P.M., as opposed to the bar across the street that served alcohol and not much else into the wee hours?

I read an opinion into the record that was short on bullshit and long on telling it like it was. I realized while I was announcing my ruling that I was angry, and it showed. But I rather imagine that God gets plenty angry at some of the rank injustices we perpetrate on each other and I'm sure he does not hesitate to make his displeasure known.

Two weeks later, Annie got her new lease. Shortly thereafter, the town got a new mayor.

· · · · · ·

After six months, my law clerks and I drove quietly into the little town, just to see how things had worked out. Annie's restaurant was open for business. Several Hispanic-looking men were eating inside, quietly and respectably. The antiques dealer who testified at the hearing had indeed moved, but the baby furniture store that replaced him appeared to be thriving. And the bar across the street had a new name, a new exterior, and a new, family-style menu. It seemed a peaceable kingdom.

That day, I felt the way I imagine God feels when the meek inherit the earth and those who are persecuted for justice come into the Kingdom of Heaven. I felt like I had done something more than interpret the law—I had given justice. It was a terrific feeling.

I have not come to abolish the law, but to fulfill it.

—Matthew 5:17

LAWYERS CAN BE FORGIVEN for feeling a little disrespected by the New Testament. The scribes (lawyers) are second only to the Pharisees in bearing the brunt of Jesus' contempt. They—we—are cursed for being hypocrites. They—we—are accused of neglecting justice, mercy and faith (Mt 23:23). They—we—are accused of loading God's chosen people with burdens too hard to bear (Lk 11:46). Paul takes the matter one step further, going on and on about how the children of the promise have trumped the children of the law. What are we modern-day children of the law supposed to think of ourselves?

And in light of all this rancor and contempt, what are we to think of that strange punch line to the Sermon on the Mount—Jesus' pronouncement that he came, not to abolish the law, but to fulfill it? "Fulfill" means "to bring into actuality," "to measure up to" and "to satisfy or complete." But the word "law" as used in the Gospels suggests a tool of oppression. How can the One who offers an end to all oppression be its fulfillment?

I struggle with the seeming inconsistency of these texts as I sit on my own little Gabbatha and try to make vocational sense of what I do. And I come up with this.

Distilled to its essence, Jesus' message is that, in everything we do, we are to follow two simple commandments—Love God with everything in you, and love your neighbor as yourself. The greatest commandments, he called them. The essence of the law. Let them guide all your endeavors and voilà—the law suddenly measures up to what it is supposed to be. It becomes complete. It is fulfilled. In his own lifetime, Jesus managed to set a pretty fair example of how it was supposed to work.

We, of course, are Jesus' hands and feet in today's world. So it's up to us to carry on the work of fulfilling the law. We have to finish what he started, by bringing into actuality a law that reflects the two great commandments.

If this is what it means for Jesus to be the fulfillment of the law, then I see a glimmer of hope for humanity. I see it in the progression of our own laws, the very laws that American lawyers and judges are sworn to uphold. Our country's laws are far from perfect, but we aspire to make them so. Each generation, through trial and error and no little struggle, has carved away some of the bits and pieces of the law of this land that do not reflect love of God and neighbor. In so doing, we are fulfilling the law. We are creeping, oh so slowly but oh so deliberately, toward a law that measures up to itself—the law of love.

Already we have covered much ground on our journey. We no longer have laws on the books that allow some people to own other people, that deny whole classes of people the full rights of citizenship, that permit the exploitation of children or the harassment of minorities in the workplace. It is no longer the law of this land that separate is equal, that acts of violence can be ignored because they occur in a home rather than on the street, or that you have to own property to cast your ballot. Most twenty-first-century Americans hold these truths to be self-evident. But if we need to remind ourselves that they are not (and from time to time we *should* remind ourselves that they are not), we need only look at dozens of other societies on this small planet—or backwards in time, to an earlier version of our own—where the wickedness of such things is not, or was not, transparent.

When I became a judge I swore to defend the Constitution and laws of the United States against all enemies, foreign and domestic. I think I understand what that means. It means that I uphold the law, come what may, without regard to public opinion or the prevailing political winds or my own personal preferences. "If you have ever fantasized about being a member of Congress and making laws, now is not the time to act out your fantasy," I tell jurors at the end of every trial. In admonishing them not to nullify the law, I admonish myself as well. If I am true to my oath, I do not have the luxury of taking a Chinese menu approach to the law—enforcing the statutes I agree with and discarding the rest. Of course, I get to interpret the law, but within the confines of pretty clearly articulated rules of construction: following the decisions of higher courts, for example, and giving primacy to the expressed intentions of the lawmakers. If there should come a time when, having interpreted a law, I cannot in good conscience enforce it, then I believe that I would have but one choice—to resign my office. I flatter myself that I would have taken such a course rather than enforce certain laws that were once very much a part of the legal landscape—Jim Crow laws, for example, or poll taxes that limited suffrage. Fortunately for me I have not yet been put to so harsh a test. It is possible that the test will come. But that is far less likely to happen than it would have been one hundred, or even fifty, years ago. Such is the happy consequence of our American march toward the fulfillment of the law.

I mark something else as I contemplate these things. The visionaries in our country who agitate for new and better laws are, for the most part, lawyers. The legislators who midwife those more perfect laws into being are mostly lawyers. The men and women who use laws to attack wrongdoing and inequity in our society are usually lawyers. The people who make sure that those who are entitled to the protection of the law get it are lawyers. The litigators who challenge laws that do not reflect the ideals on which our country was founded are lawyers. And the judges who apply the laws impartially to resolve the disputes among our citizens are lawyers. Many of those lawyers are people of faith; some of those people of faith follow Jesus as Lord. A few of them might think in theological terms; if they do, they may understand that they are part of a long march toward the fulfillment of the Great Commandments. Most probably do not think in such terms. But there is no doubt in my mind that they are.

To such men and women of the law, I say do not dwell inordinately on outdated evangelical criticism of our profession. From where I sit, I see that we have a great deal to be proud of. Oh, the work is not over. It will never be over until the law is perfect, and nothing human can ever be perfect. But perhaps aspiring toward perfection is more important than attaining it. After all, in the beginning, when God looked at creation, he did not see that it was perfect. He saw that it was good. In the beginning, it seems, good was good enough. Turning the good into the perfect must be the reason we were created.